P9-EGJ-921

THE PEOPLE OF JAPAN

by Pearl S. Buck

PHOTOGRAPHS BY STUART FOX

SIMON AND SCHUSTER · NEW YORK

PUBLISHED BY SIMON AND SCHUSTER
ROCKEFELLER CENTER, 630 FIFTH AVENUE
NEW YORK, NEW YORK 10020
FIRST PRINTING
LIBRARY OF CONGRESS CATALOG CARD NUMBER: 66–20246
DESIGNED BY HELEN BARROW
MANUFACTURED IN THE UNITED STATES OF AMERICA
LETTERPRESS BY AMERICAN BOOK–STRATFORD PRESS, INC.
OFFSET BY DUENEWALD-KONECKY LITHOGRAPHERS, INC.
BINDING BY AMERICAN BOOK–STRATFORD PRESS, INC., NEW YORK

CONCEIVED BY LYLE KENYON ENGEL

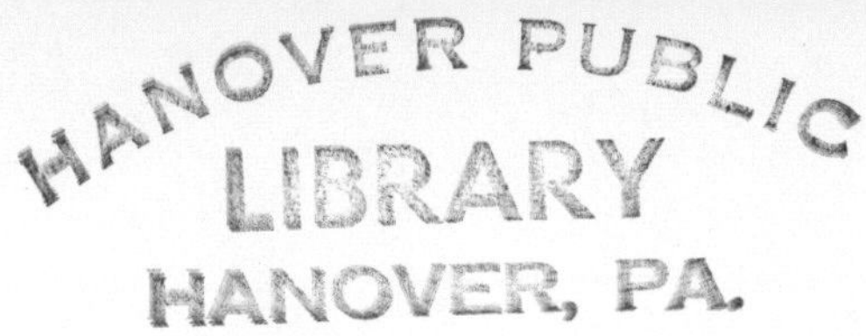

We wish to acknowledge the cooperation of General Aniline & Film Corporation which supplied the Super Hypan® and Versapan® black-and-white film and the Anscochrome® color transparency film on which all pictures of *The People of Japan* were made. We are grateful to Shriro Trading Co., Ltd. (Japan) for their cooperation in processing this film for reproduction in the book. We also wish to acknowledge the cooperation of E. Yamanaka, Export Manager of Nippon Kogaku (Japan) and Joseph Ehrenreich of Nikon, Inc. (U.S.A.) for making available their Nikon cameras and lenses.

Special thanks to the Nissan Motor Co., Ltd. for the use of their Datsun sedan and to the British Overseas Airways Corporation for their excellent service and unlimited cooperation.

Sincerest appreciation to Marla Ray, Valerie Moolman and George Engel for their assistance on this book.

—P. S. B.

THE PEOPLE OF JAPAN

I

LONG BEFORE I was born the people of Japan were a part of my world, a part of my family history. My parents, as intrepid and adventurous a pair as ever lived, embarked for China in the year 1880, my mother a bride of twenty-three, my father a missionary idealist of twenty-eight. Japan was their first sight of the Orient. Their ship stopped at three ports, Yokohama, Kobe and Nagasaki. Knowing my parents, I am sure they went ashore and as far inland as possible, taking in all available sights for further reflection. Whatever these first impressions may have been, they gave the two young Americans a false notion of the rest of Asia, the Asia where they were to spend their lives. For if there is one single truth about Asia, it is that while each country there is totally different from every other, Japan is the most different of all. Her people are unique, even among Asian peoples, and this in spite of the fact that there are two centers in Asia: India and China, the two mother cultures. Each of the other Asian countries is influenced to some degree, in spite of differences, by one of the two great ones. Japan, however, being an island nation, is the least influenced by juxtaposition, and the most independent in her adaptations.

My parents, therefore, were innocently deceived by what they saw of old Japan. What did they see? Enough to enchant them! Those were the days of Japan's untouched and original beauty. True, her sons had traveled to the Asian continent, for as early as the seventh century Japan was adapting foreign ways to her own people. Before that time, for example, the Japanese had had no written language of their own. When they discovered the beautiful and rich language of the Chinese, they borrowed the ideographs but used them for the totally different Japanese spoken language. Japan's religion, too, was originally an amorphous mass of folklore. Then Buddhism came to her from India through China and Korea, and the Japanese people modified its tenets to suit themselves. As historian George Sansom puts it in his *Japan: A Short Cultural History,* Japan found Buddhism, as expressed in China, "a religion excellent for protecting the State." Finding it useful, the Japanese used it in a way peculiarly their own. They adapted it according to their needs; they built great Buddhist temples and monasteries after the Chinese pattern, thereby influencing their own architecture permanently.

But in spite of all their adaptations from other countries and cultures, the Japanese maintained their own national character. They did not change to accommodate the new elements they brought home from abroad. On the contrary, they did and do change the new to accommodate their own unchanging selves. Thus today, when one travels in Japan, a country as modern as any in the West, it is not to find the Japanese people greatly changed. In fact, the longer one stays in Japan the more apparent it is that the Japanese people are basically unchanged, in spite of their very modern appearance and way of living.

Let me interject here that when I came to my own country to live, after spending the first half of my life in Asia, I was unhappy to see that Americans understood Japan so little as to say, carelessly, that the Japanese were imitators of others. Nothing could be further from the truth, now or ever. The people of Japan have been searchers and discoverers of the best in every culture. Whatever they have learned they have not used imitatively but creatively, taking what was useful to their way of life, changing and adapting and making anew. Their culture is an admirable blend of the best in other cultures and the indigenous culture of her own people. The same search goes on, resulting in a Japan which is in step with all that is most modern everywhere in the world.

This is her genius, today as it has always been. Take, for example again, the influence of China. Although the early Japanese travelers saw much to admire in ancient China, although her architecture, her art, her calligraphy, even her dress, were brought back and adapted for the people of Japan, yet China's casteless society was not brought back; her system of government, so solidly based upon democratic principles, was not brought back, nor was the cool philosophical intellectualism of Confucian ethics. Official titles in China were given to those men who had passed the imperial examinations, but in Japan such titles were hereditary and feudal and continued so. Moreover, Japan never renewed her national health by a change of dynasty as China did.

My parents, therefore, were not prepared for China by their early introduction to Japan. When they arrived in China, it was, I confess, to judge the great sprawling population of continental China as more than a little dismaying. To that extent Japan remained for them somewhat of a dream country, a land of disciplined beauty, of cleanliness and order, a land of manageability and comprehensibility, let us say, in contrast to the geographic vastness and traditional profundities of China. To Japan my parents escaped in later years for brief periods when torrid summers and contending warlords made China intolerable.

I had, therefore, to make my own approach to Japan, and in my own generation. In childhood terms, visiting there as we came and went across the Pacific, Japan was for me, too, a dream country. The beautiful landscape, the mannered architecture, the gaily dressed people, always smiling, always polite, always bearing gifts for a child, presented a storybook quality. I used to look forward to those stops in Japan, and the more because the islands made a harbor of safety and serenity in the endless storm-ridden sea surrounding them. Instinctively I took refuge there years later with my own family when the Communists attacked Nanking, where we were living.

"Let us go to Japan," I said then, as my parents had said before me, and thither we went, the four of us. We rented a small Japanese house in the mountains above Nagasaki, near the hot springs of Unzen, and there we lived until China was safe for us again—though only for a few years at that, for the vicissitudes of history gave the victory to the Communists, after all.

In the years that I lived in Japan, waiting for the return to my Chinese home, I went as deeply perhaps as a Westerner can into the life and thought of the Japanese people. First let me say here and now that I love them. I inherited love for them from my parents, love for old Japan and old Japanese ways. Upon the solid foundation of love I discovered them through many years, and do still continue to discover, with each new visit and each new approach.

II

In the old days the approach was by ship and today it is by air. Hovering downward out of the sky, I see that the people of Japan live upon a crescent of islands, stretching farther to the north than to the south, and that they are all far out in the Pacific Ocean. Why this geographical observation? Because one must know the contour of the country, its relation to other countries and to the surrounding seas, its position on the globe. All of these seemingly external facts are in reality pertinent to the people living in that country. Island peoples, for example, are very different from continental peoples. Island people whose island is near a continent are different from those dwelling upon islands isolated by the ocean. The Japanese, then, are a geographically isolated people, and it is axiomatic that they should have developed their own national character. One is bound to find differences between them and other peoples, contradictions between them and not only Westerners but other Asian peoples as well.

But the contradictions, the differences, are not only international. Within Japan's own islands there are contrasts. Her land expanse is divided into four large islands, surrounded by many smaller ones. The four main islands are Hokkaido in the extreme north; Honshu, the largest island; Shikoku, south across the Inland Sea from Honshu; and Kyushu, the southernmost island and perhaps the most beautiful, where Nagasaki is situated. Into these four islands and the surrounding cluster of small ones are crowded the people of Japan, 96,160,000 as of 1963.

It is natural that the people on the four main islands should be more modern, more open to change, than those on the islands remote from the lanes of travel by sea and air. To know by inference what old Japan was like one must visit the little islands where the people still wear kimono and geta, and where the permanent wave has not afflicted the heads of the women. I consider it one of the less happy influences invading Japan, the permanent wave! The hair of Japanese women was once so beautiful, long, straight, lustrous. Today, except in remote areas, it is crinkled, dry, rusty and burnt, and usually short. I say boldly that this sort of hair does not suit Japanese faces.

Yes, on the smaller islands one still sees the old Japan, and on the larger ones the new. Yet even among the four main islands there are differences and contradictions. For example, the people on the northernmost island, Hokkaido, are an Aryan people, the Ainu, now almost extinct except on this island, the Kurile Islands, and in certain parts of Sakhalin. They are light-skinned, their eyes are pale, and they are hairy in contrast to the smooth-skinned Japanese. Anthropologically they are Caucasian, and in ancient times there was much strife between the Ainu and the other people of Japan. Once they must have spread over all the islands, as evidenced by the Ainu names found everywhere in Japan. The name of Mount Fuji, for example, which legend tells us rose up in one night, leaving a great depression known now as Lake Biwa, is basically Ainu, Fuji in Ainu meaning "fire." The Goddess of Fire is a household deity among the Ainu, who worship fire, sun, wind and stars, the ocean and other natural phenomena, all in a primitive sort of fashion. Among animals they worship the bear, whom also they eat as part of their ceremonial worship, provided he is at the right stage of plumpness and tenderness. They have no written language and their history is all told from generation to generation. They work at fishing and farming for livelihood and now raise much of Japan's cattle.

Their island, second largest among the four, is so different from the rest of Japan that it seems almost another country. In a land that is for the most part uncomfortably, almost unbelievably crowded, Hokkaido is a spacious isle. It has only five per cent of Japan's population, but twenty-one per cent of her land area. It boasts the largest national park, Daisetsuzan, 573,000 acres, one of Japan's largest rivers, the Ishikari, which runs for more than 200 miles before it empties into the sea of Japan, vast forests, big dairy farms, big sheep farms, rich fishing grounds, many volcanoes, many hot springs; almost an extravagance of space and riches. Neither is the climate typical of Japan, for Hokkaido is a region as cold as Canada, in comparison to Honshu's mildness and Kyushu's semitropic heat. It has much to offer both visitor and immigrant from the other isles, yet even today it experiences no great influx of those who hunger for variety and space or of those who would bring great changes to it.

Yet there has of course been some modernization of life on Hokkaido. American engineers and agricultural experts have helped to change the face of its vast wilderness into forest reserves and modern farms; educators, Americans among them, have given their services to Hokkaido's youth. American Professor William S. Clark is well known for his work in the University of Hokkaido at Sapporo, and known with such honor that a fifteen-foot granite pillar has been erected to him about half way between the airport and the city itself. On the pillar is a bronze plaque, green with age, and on the plaque we see the bearded face of Clark, and the date, April 10,1877, and the Horatio Alger words, "Boys, be ambitious." It seems that these were Clark's last words as he left Hokkaido, surrounded by thousands of grieving students. It seems, too, that the boys *were* ambitious, for many of Clark's students, and their sons after them, have become leaders in national affairs. But the great majority of the people of Hokkaido have been slow to welcome change.

The people of the southernmost island, Kyushu, are very different, although they are also fisherfolk and farmers. They have, of course, been more open to modern influences, for Kyushu, unlike Hokkaido, has long been in the sea lanes of ocean liners. Kyushu is my favorite among the islands of Japan, and this because of its rich variety—or perhaps because I have twice spent long periods of my life there, the last only recently. Her people are warm and friendly and impetuous. Their language has an Irish sort of brogue, although Japanese, of course, and one can always tell where a man or woman comes from by that tang and tangle of the tongue.

Kyushu is perhaps most famous for its many hot springs, the best known of which are at Beppu. Among these springs there are six main ones, known as "hells." Boiling mud, boiling water, over four hundred feet deep, cool lakes full of crocodiles, lakes as red as blood, geysers of steaming hot water, all can be seen at Beppu, for the town is floating on a sea of hot water that lies a few feet beneath the surface. Here, too, are the baths of hot sand, where one may bury oneself to the neck and be pervaded by the heat of the earth.

There are two large cities on the island, Fukuoka and Nagasaki. Fukuoka is a city of parks and shrines and popular festivals. Nagasaki is Kyushu's chief port and I remember it well from my earliest days, for it was always our ship's last stop before we disembarked in Shanghai. In those days it was a quiet little city, smelling of dried fish and old warehouses, or godowns as they were called. I remember how, when I was so small that I clung to my father's big bony hand, I found the cobbled streets difficult for my slippered feet, and yet the walk was worthwhile, for we always bought a special kind of yellow sponge cake there, and we always went to see the house where Puccini is said to have written, or at least conceived the idea of writing, *Madame Butterfly*.

Many memories cling about that city. On the mountains above it, in the coolness of bamboos and Buddhist temples, my parents used to go for the summers, and upon the return one summer, long before I was born, my sister Maude died at sea at the age of six months and was buried in the Christian cemetery in Shanghai. And it was to those same hills, as I have said earlier, that I went for refuge from Chinese Communists. Between those early and later years there were two world wars, in both of which Japan took part. At the end of the second, an atomic bomb was dropped upon Nagasaki. The beautiful old port was partly destroyed, and now it has been rebuilt after a fashion. Madame Butterfly's house is still there, rather drab as crowds of Japanese tourists tramp through its empty rooms.

That last visit to Nagasaki was sad. I went to the memorial built on the spot where the bomb fell. I saw men and women there, standing with bowed heads, wreaths in their hands to lay for the dead. We did not speak. What was there to say, except words of useless regret?

It is no wonder that the old atmosphere is gone. I found

the memory of it one afternoon when I went to visit an old friend, herself a sort of Madame Butterfly in her beautiful youth. Her lover had been a Dutch merchant and he married her and built her a fine house overlooking the bay. She traveled with him in those early days and he was proud to show her off to his fellow merchants in Europe. Now he is dead, the house is falling into ruins, and she lives on alone with the remnant of what had once been there. She set the tea table for me and we drank tea from beautiful cracked cups. The tablecloth was of fine old Brussels lace, darned into a delicate cobweb. We sat on her shaky veranda and faced her untended garden as we talked of old times, of things that had forever changed.

But Kyushu has not changed too much, if one leaves the cities. The countryside is as lovely as ever in the mild climate, the hills as green, the terraced fields as lush. The newest sight is the school children, all in Western dress, all with knapsacks and thermos bottles, on their way to school. They are everywhere, in city and countryside, and it is evident that they are considered Japan's most valued national treasure.

The mountains also are the same. With a Japanese friend, I was driven up the same winding, perilous roads to the hot springs resort of Unzen. Outside that town, across a narrow gorge, upon a mountainside, stood the small Japanese house in which we had once taken refuge. It was all of wood, its front was shoji which could open the entire house to the forest, and my kitchen was a clay pot of burning charcoal on the back porch. A tiny bathroom was behind the porch, its only furniture a wooden tub. I remember that one morning, happening to be in the tub, I chanced to glance at a knothole in the outer wall of the room and saw applied there an eye, intent and black. I thrust my forefinger into the knothole, and the eye withdrew. When I was dressed, I went outside to find the possessor of the eye. It belonged to an old woman who had come to sell fresh crabs. We laughed together, and she paid me a few compliments. She is of the Japan that does not, will not, change, for her like is still in the countryside and villages of Kyushu.

I spent four happy months in the pretty little town of Obama not long ago. I lived in a Japanese inn, ate Japanese rice, fresh fish and crabs, and lived the life of Japan, and a delightful life it is. If you do not know Obama you have missed an essential part of Japan. It is a resort, I suppose, but not a showy one. Hot springs provide medicinal baths, and the naturally hot water is also pumped into the hotel. I had a delightful room opening on a private veranda that overlooked a huge hot-water pool. Beyond was the sea. Down a flight of steps was my own luxurious bath, a large room with tiled floor and a small sunken pool for a tub. Everyone knows, of course, that one does not in Japan simply step into the tub. A scrupulous scrubbing precedes that pleasure. Soap and brush and a wooden pail wait near at hand, the pail to dip water from the tub and wash off soap. Only then may one enjoy the hot water—very hot—in the tub.

What pure physical joy it was, after a long hard day, to come back and soak away all weariness in that hot beneficent water! And after the bath came the quiet meal alone in my own room, the low table set with bowl and chopsticks, a lacquered box of hot rice, a small fish or a big crab, some delicately prepared vegetables. The little maid in her bright kimono knelt to serve me as I sat on the tatami floor. And after the meal, she removed the dishes and put aside the table and then drew out of the wall closets the mattresses and quilts. Outside my veranda people were laughing and splashing in the big pool. In another part of my life, when I was not alone, I might have been annoyed by the shouts and laughter of the bathers, but not now. It was a comfort to hear human voices so near and especially to hear human gaiety. At midnight, after the guests were in their rooms asleep, a group of ten or twelve young men swam nude in the pool. Sometimes, sleepless, I rose to watch them. They made a lovely sight, their slim young bodies pale in the moonlight.

What I really want to remember and to tell is my return visit to Unzen. They do not forget their friends, those charming people of Unzen. For example, let me remember the afternoon when I decided to visit there, where more than thirty years earlier I had taken refuge from Chinese Communists to live in the small Japanese house.

I wanted to see it again and renew my memories. A kind Japanese friend went with me. We hired a small car with a reckless young driver and whirled up the narrow curving mountain road. The road winds in and out of the folded mountains, revealing at every turn glimpses of the sea far below. Unzen, or Paradise in the Clouds, lies 2,400 feet above the sea, and the highest mountain reaches 4,500 feet. The surrounding region is a national park, famous for azaleas in the spring, bright foliage in the autumn, and magnificent cedars. It was, I saw as we hurtled up and around the curves, as lovely as ever. But I was astonished to see how Unzen itself had grown. I remembered it as a small village set in the midst of steaming hot springs and rocks from whose crevices issued spirals of hot mists. We used to join the Japanese tourists and boil eggs and rice over those natural caldrons. Now, three decades later, Unzen is a modern spa, great hotels looming against the sky and busy modern streets.

I was lost and did not know how to find my way to the gorge and the little house in the pine forest. Quite by chance, I stopped a young girl and put my question to her.

"Do you know anyone who could remember an American family, refugees from China in 1927?"

She was not at all surprised. "Oh, yes," she said brightly. "My grandfather knew them."

She produced the grandfather, a spry thin little old man who led us out of town to the narrow gorge. We crossed it on foot by the same rickety bridge I remembered, and there saw the house. It was empty and closed, but it was there and, staying there for a while, I was satisfied and ready to leave it forever.

When we parted, I insisted upon giving the old man a small gift of money, which he refused, and then under pressure unwillingly accepted. He had his way, however, as Japanese usually do, somehow. Before our car left town we heard a voice calling us. It was the young girl, in her hands a package. We stopped.

"Grandfather wants you to have these rice cakes," she panted, out of breath. "He says you used to buy them for your children."

Long ago I had forgotten, but now I remembered. It was quite true that I had bought the rice cakes, crisp and delicious. But the old man had not forgotten. Is it surprising that I find the Japanese lovable?

SHIKOKU, TOO, holds memories for me, less personal perhaps, but pleasant. I have not lived on this smallest of Japan's main islands, but I have crossed the island-dotted Inland Sea on the little liners that leave Osaka and Kobe to thread their way across the placid waters, and have seen its untamed loveliness. All Japan has natural beauty, but this island has special interest for those who seek to know the country and its people in their play as well as their work.

The trip itself is a delight. Hundreds of tiny islands fleck the waters over an area of three hundred miles, comprising a sort of gigantic water garden known as the Inland Sea National Park. The calm and mirror-like sea, its surface gently broken by paths of steamers and the little fishing boats that ply their way between the isles, reflects mist-fringed shores and purple mountain peaks. Always I found on board the spirit of camaraderie so characteristic of the Japanese when on a holiday trip. Laughing, chattering people, I remember, would line the deck rails, pointing out strips of beautiful white beach and green pine groves, and talking proudly of the wonders of their special island. And Shikoku is indeed both beautiful and unique.

On this island, for example, are made the famous puppets for the puppet plays, the Bunraku, four-foot-high figures expertly devised and manipulated so that body, limbs, hands, head, mouth, eyes, and even eyebrows, move. Three men are required to handle each doll, so many are the moving parts. In addition to the manipulators, there is also the *taiu* to narrate the play, and the samisen player to evoke mood through musical notes. Puppet plays are not given on Shikoku or its satellite islands, though. The city of Osaka on Honshu is the permanent home of the Bunraku. The Bunrakuza Theater there is devoted exclusively to puppet plays, and traveling groups only occasionally take the plays to other parts of the country.

On Shikoku one also finds the dogs who are bred for fighting. They are dressed in actual imitation of the corpulent *sumo* wrestlers so admired by the Japanese, wearing loin cloths and a knot of hair on their heads. Fighting bulls are another specialty of the island, but the bulls are trained to fight each other, not men. The Japanese do not believe in pitting unequals one against the other.

One finds here, too, the famous long-tailed roosters called *naga-o-dori,* a fowl that possesses a tail that is beautiful but impractical, since it is encouraged to grow to a length of more than twenty feet. Careful cross-breeding between common fowl and less common pheasant produces the result. These magnificent birds are classed as national treasures by the beauty-loving Japanese, and treated with a care appropriate to the most exotic and delicate of creatures. The birds do not fight; they do not even exercise without the help of three attendants to hold up their flowing trains. They are bred only for their beauty.

Startlingly different is the neighboring island of Honshu, to the north across the Inland Sea, which contains the world-famous capital, Tokyo. It is now as usual to visit Tokyo as Paris or London. I remember it in my youth as a rather remote place, not busy like Yokohama, the seaport, or Osaka, the business center. There was a great hue and cry in those days when Frank Lloyd Wright built the Imperial Hotel, much argument about its architecture, still more about its being built upon a platform of pine pilings floating in a sea of mud. It was then considered modern and strange, a sort of world wonder. Now in new Tokyo it seems old-fashioned. Yet it has survived earthquake and war.

Today's Tokyo strikes the newcomer like a blow. It is noisy, crowded, new and blaring, the largest city in the world both in area and population, and still growing. A pity, I think, after it was all but destroyed by bombing, that it could not have been planned and designed to become a beautiful city, with that happy combination of old and new which is so truly Japanese. For it was most cruelly bombed during the war, the reason for this being that munitions were made by many families throughout the city and not in central factories. Parts were made in such scattered places and diversified forms that often the workers themselves did not know what they were making. So dispersed was the work that target bombing was impossible, and the city was therefore bombed as an entity.

In theory, it would have been possible to redesign and rebuild it in its entirety. After the war, however, pressures were such that shops and offices went up almost overnight, according to economic necessity, without regard to beauty or even convenience. In the haste to bring back normal conditions, people and industries built as they could. The result is the considerable confusion of a great sprawling town in which many of the streets are unnamed and the most modern vies with the old. One may stop at a modern hotel or an old inn, shop in the world's most enormous department stores or sip green tea in an age-old ceremony. An hour's drive takes one out of the metropolis, which is equal to any great city of the West, and one finds the ancient countryside of old Japan.

One finds that ancient countryside, I may say, a good deal more easily than one finds the average Tokyo street address. As I have said, many of the streets are unnamed, but that is only part of the difficulty. Most of the houses are unnumbered. The houses that do have numbers have not been numbered consecutively, but rather according to the order in which they were built. Thus, on any street—usually itself a capriciously twisting, haphazard affair—House Number 3 may be next to House Number 57; and in any district, House Number 2 may be a mile away from House Number 1. This is not something that is due to the war. It was ever thus. Usually a Japanese host will send a car to pick up his guests. Or he will draw a detailed map consisting largely of landmarks and advise you to show this to your taxi driver. Your taxi driver will take one look at your map and drive off with great confidence and noise. When he has reached top speed he will turn around and cheerfully ask you where to go next. Your ride then becomes a series of stops and starts, of friendly conversations on street corners and amiable discussions of possible routes. Everyone offers helpful suggestions: the policeman from his corner box, the mailman on his rounds, the storekeeper, the housewife, the passing cyclist, the businessman on his way home from work. Eventually you reach your destination, late but warmly welcome. No one is surprised, no one minds. They all know what a maze their city is, and in a way they seem almost proud. It is part of Tokyo's character.

I might mention here that the police and public officials of Japan are uniformly courteous. I have always found them to be most gracious and polite under even the most trying circumstances. Now that there are ten million people in Tokyo and a constant swarm of tourists, their task can seldom be easy. Yet their patience is never-ending.

One's total impression of the city is that of a cosmopolitan, modern metropolis. Its people are lively, busy, prosperous, well dressed. In the Japan I knew in the years before the war the citizens wore kimono and walked in geta. Today they wear Western dress, their shoes are leather, and kimono and geta are reserved for private or formal wear. The variety of people on the street is diverting and amazing. Any amusement, any industry can be found here. Taxicabs, buses and bicycles crowd the streets, and speed is the order of the day. Tokyo is the great, fast-beating heart through whose arteries flows the blood of a nation and a people.

III

WHO ARE these people of Japan? They are a complex, a melting pot, a mélange of peoples, originally from the north Asian mainland and Malaysian islands, the remoteness of whose chosen country gave them time to become unified and develop their own civilization. Because the Japanese are an island people they have developed insularity. Island peoples do; even the British have not been able to escape it. And yet they are separated from the Continent only by a narrow strait, whereas Japan is separated from her neighbor, Korea, by a body of water six times as wide.

Even as continental peoples share their own peculiar nature, so do island peoples. There are, for example, the same similarities between Britain and Japan that exist between China and the United States, two continental peoples. That is to say, Americans are more like Chinese, barring Communism, than they are like Japanese or English. The very attitude toward life among island peoples is different from that of continental peoples. Island peoples are at the same time more reserved and yet less calm than continental peoples. I make the arbitrary statement, but I believe history bears it out. The fact of having space in which to expand breeds calm. Nature is kinder, too, upon a continent. At least there is more chance of escaping storm and violence. There is always somewhere to go.

At the same time, contradictorily, island peoples are seafaring and expansive. Their horizons are near and, confined within their narrow shores, they feel compelled to wander. Empire tempts them; certainly it tempted Britain and Japan, and this independently, for as early as the sixteenth century Japan dreamed of Asian empire, and especially of China. It was Hideyoshi of Japan who besought his emperor to allow him to sail forth with a great fleet of wooden ships to conquer China, his only request being that when he had achieved victory he be rewarded by being made viceroy of China. Whether he could have achieved such heights cannot be known, since he went by way of Korea and there was vanquished by Admiral Yi, who devised the first ironclad ships of war, and by means of burning arrows released through holes in the iron destroyed the Japanese fleet.

Japanese ambitions broke forth again in 1894 in the form of a fresh attack on China. In this war Russia was the mediator, claiming as her reward the Maritime Provinces of China and the warm water port of Vladivostok. In the First World War, then with the Allies, Japan had secured her foothold on the Chinese mainland by taking from Germany the lands she held in China, and, with characteristic determination, she set forth again for empire, seizing Manchuria before the Second World War. In short, the aims and ambitions of Japan have been in character with her island people, a close-knit and insular society and yet one impelled toward expansion.

The Japanese people have been isolated by more than geography, however. They have been isolated, sometimes for centuries, by their own government's policy against outsiders. This, too, is an island trait. I suppose island peoples, knowing they have no place of retreat if they are attacked, do tend to prevent the arrival of strangers. Beautifully courteous as the Japanese always are when visitors arrive, they do not easily receive us into their homes and lives. This was a matter for private pain when I was a child, for Japanese children are friendly and adorable and I longed to know them better. It was only when I grew older that I realized that what seemed to be withdrawal was the result of national fear and determination—fear of the monstrously encroaching West and determination not to be engulfed as other Asian countries had been.

Let me be specific. It is difficult for Western peoples to understand the distrust that Asian peoples manifest toward us today. Americans, especially, are hurt by it. We give gifts, we send missionaries, we pour out money in aid, we send food, we offer technological advice and trade—and find ourselves the least loved of all peoples and the most feared, generally speaking.

Why? If we have read history, we should not be surprised, nor even ask the question, for the answer is there. Centuries ago the Asian nations were visited by men from Portugal, Spain and Italy, from Holland and France—white men. They came in ships, seeking trade. Indeed, such trade was essential to their lives. They needed spices for their food. Without the preservative qualities of spices, meat, their staple fare, quickly became uneatable. Overland trade routes had long been established through the Middle East, but when that territory fell under the rule of Muslim conquerors, such routes were closed. It then became necessary to find routes by sea. Portugal was the first to round the continent of Africa and to reach India.

Other ships followed, ships from many nations. Unprepared for invasion, the Asian countries soon found themselves entangled in foreign empires. The process was simple, forceful and invariable. The preliminary purpose always was trade. For the less cultivated European peoples, Asia was a treasure house. Traders found local conditions complex, however, and Asian governments uncooperative. Moreover, laws, East and West, were different. Capital punishment was intolerable for a European or Englishman when the crime was no crime by Western law. It was necessary, these men of the West declared, that they be immune to Asian laws, and that they be tried in their own Western courts. Thus, very early, an immunity granted nowadays only to diplomats became the custom and finally the right of all white people living or visiting in Asia. This immunity was called extraterritoriality. It meant that white men could do whatever they pleased, and they did so with the result that throughout centuries an immense resentment mounted against all white people, and continues now as a residue of history.

When laws could be disregarded, trade was insisted upon, and by force. Three times, for example, England went to war with China, and three times her victory gave her the power to sell opium to the people of China, against the wish and law of the Chinese government. With each victory came indemnities and seizure of lands as concessions. India was taken over entirely by England, Indonesia by Holland, while France carved out a huge area from China, called Indochina, comprised of Vietnam, Laos and Cambodia. The present animosity against Americans in that part of Asia is a direct result of such episodes. We are primarily white people, and we bear the burden of history.

What has all this to do with the people of Japan today? A

great deal, for Japan remained the only Asian country entirely free from foreign rulers. This had two important effects: first, it shaped Japan's determination to remain independent by isolation; and second, it hastened her own military development, for she saw that the price of freedom was not only defense, but aggression. Thus, when Japan deliberately cut off all communication with the rest of the world, she did so for reasons which were valid from her point of view. Adventurers in all walks of life, including religion, had swarmed toward her shores, enchanted with what they discovered there. St. Francis Xavier, an early missionary, declared that of all the peoples of Asia he found the Japanese the most interesting, the most endearing. True, the Japanese, with their continuing interest in other peoples, had welcomed their visitors at first and for many years, until they discovered that missionaries and businessmen usually took over a country, the first by capturing the hearts and minds of the people, the second by gaining control over the economy. Then they surveyed their Asian neighbors and themselves, and saw the handwriting on the wall. Their government therefore closed the gates, expelled the missionaries and all but a handful of traders, and prevented further visits. On occasion they went so far as summarily to execute shipwrecked sailors.

At the same time Japan decided that she must establish her own power in Asia, her own dominance, in order to protect her own people. The decision had a profound influence upon the Japanese character. Proud and fiercely independent, the Japanese fostered a system of discipline military in its rigor, but romantic in its fanatical love of country. The roots of Japan's dichotomy lie here, I believe. From the sixteenth century, beginning with the chauvinistic dreams of Hideyoshi, leading through the war with China in 1894, the seizure of Manchuria in 1931 and the consequent Second

World War, Japan has been insular and yet aggressive, ruthless yet disciplined, cruel yet poetic and beauty-loving.

Such dichotomy has been deepened by the violence which Nature herself makes upon those islands, the unpredictability of earthquakes, typhoons and tidal waves and all dangers of sudden disaster. This has undoubtedly encouraged the people to become withdrawn, fatalistic and melancholy, with relief in moments of almost hysterical gaiety. Thus a third and perhaps most important isolation has come about as the result of their own nature, introverted, tinged with sadness and pessimism toward life. Whether the geographical and historical isolation has produced this national temperament or whether temperament has induced, at least in part, the historical aspect is a question. My own conclusion is that the geographical isolation, inevitable for many centuries before modern modes of travel were invented, in combination with the continuing perils of volcanic eruptions, tidal waves and typhoons, have profoundly influenced the Japanese mind and spirit. The violence of nature has created despair and violence in man, and the only contrasting and ameliorating forces have been those of art and some aspects of religion. All in all, Japan's history has been one of a spiritual isolation so profound that it has again and again resulted in a national claustrophobia exploding into aggression.

Yet it is only fair to view the world through Japanese eyes during the age of Western imperialism, now ended, particularly if one is to understand the Japanese of the Second World War and today. The causes for present situations are always to be discovered in the past, and one of my discoveries has been that more than any other nation the United States is responsible—directly or indirectly—for the present changes not only in Japan but in the whole of Asia. For instance, Japan's self-imposed isolation during the period of Western infiltration into Asia came to an enforced end upon the

OPPOSITE
Shimpa actress Yukiji Asaoka in her dressing room. Tokyo.

Grandmother and child. Near Nagasaki, Kyushu.

Young man.

The Japanese are a complex, a mélange of peoples...

Schoolgirls sketching. Meiji Shrine Park, Tokyo.

Business executive. Tokyo.

...and their faces reflect an amazing diversity.

Man in the street. Tokyo.

The great *kabuki* actor Baiko Onoe, backstage. Tokyo.

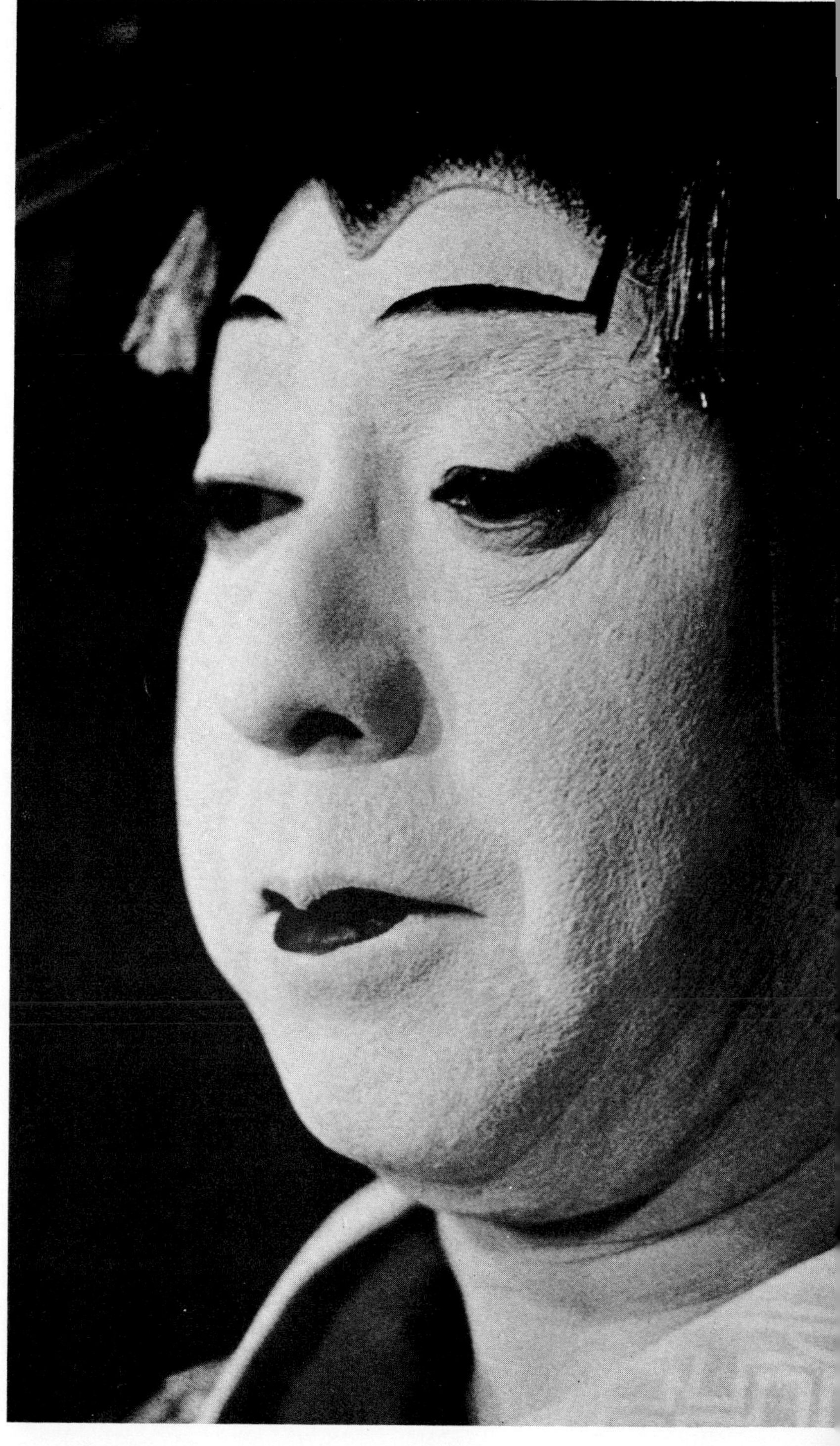

Bus stop. Aomori, Honshu.

Harvesting wheat. Hokkaido.

Truck driver and family. Northern Honshu.

The faces of youth today disclose a modern "Western" spirit—even the older generation is not untouched.

Young village girl. Northern Honshu.

Guard at the Meiji Shrine. Tokyo.

Farm worker.

Village youth.

Ladies in the afternoon. Tokyo.

Modern youth. Honshu.

Courting couple. Meiji Shrine Park, Tokyo.

Ditch digger. Northern Honshu.

Boy walking with his sister. Northern Honshu.

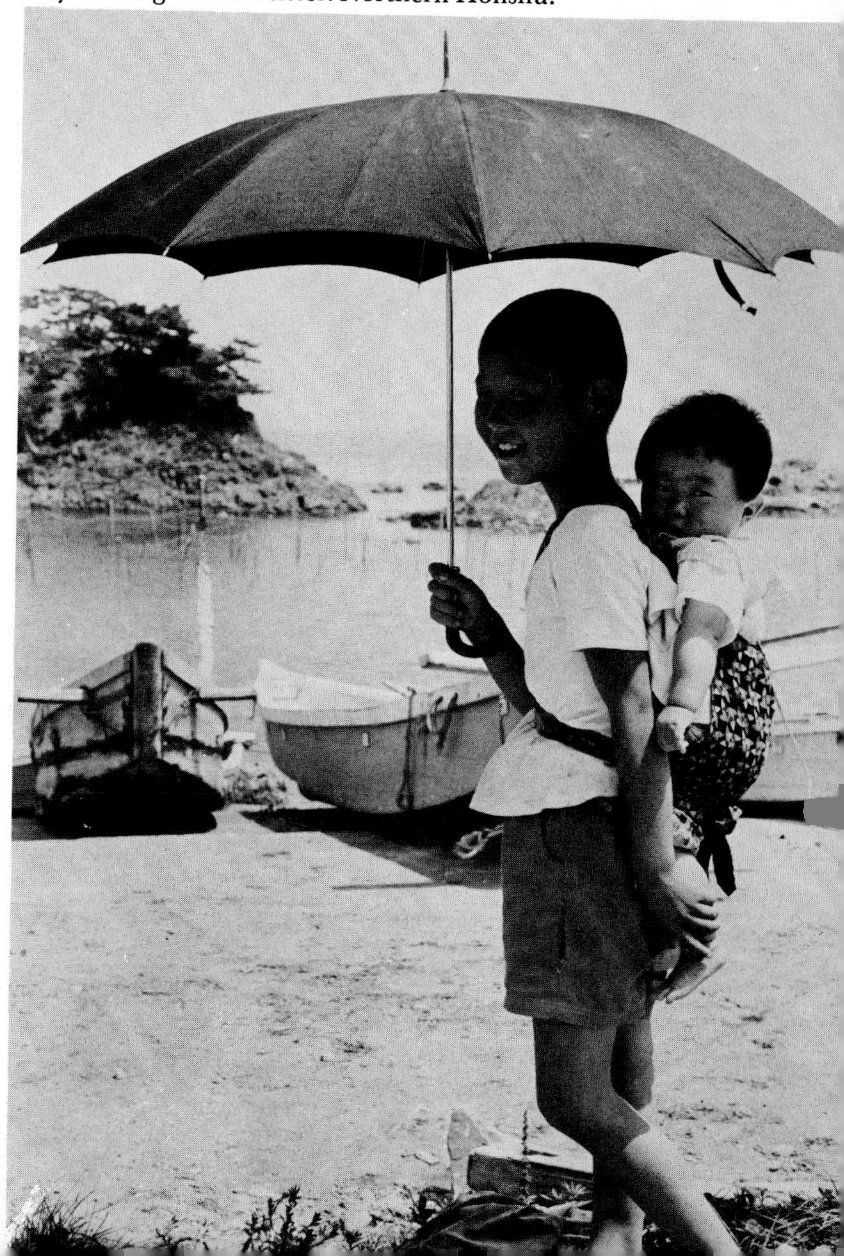

Gentleman in the park. Northern Honshu.

Yet, for all their dissimilarity...

Pearl farmer caulking pitch barrels. Northern Honshu.

Little girl reading. Honshu.

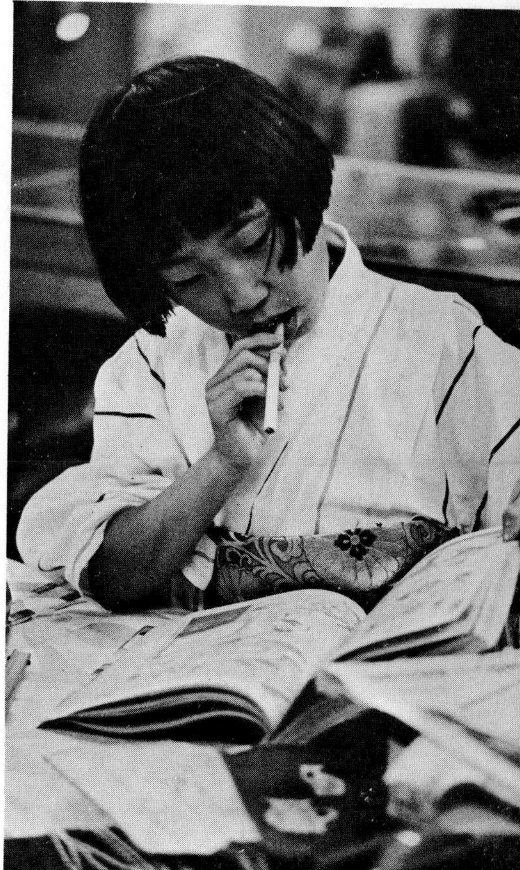

House cleaning. Tokyo.

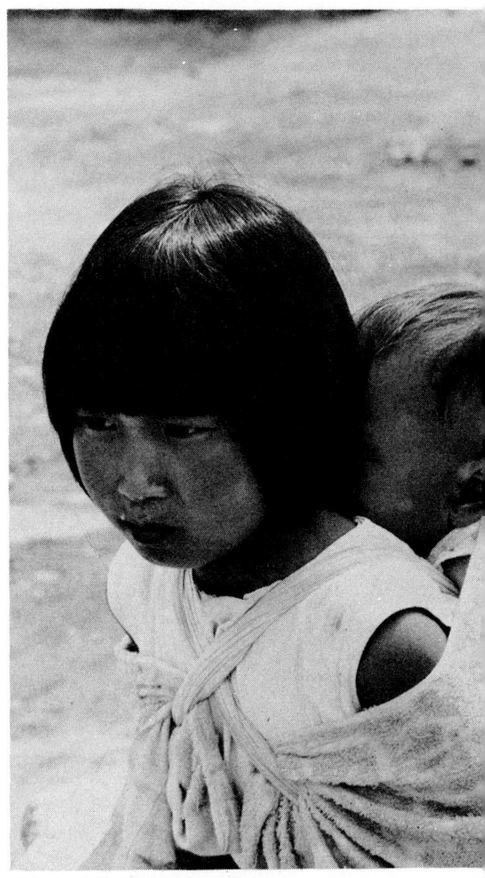

Girl with baby brother.
Iwate, Northern Honshu.

...young and old are united by a deep love of country, and enduring family traditions.

arrival of Commodore Matthew C. Perry and his fleet of black ships in the middle of the nineteenth century.

The time had come for isolation to end, the Americans declared firmly. Japan must open certain ports for the watering and fueling of American ships, and by no means were any more shipwrecked American sailors to be killed on Japanese shores. The black ships and their reputedly ferocious arms made their point. Moreover, the Japanese people were ready for change. The Tokugawa shogunate, then in power, recognized the situation. Very soon, with mutual courtesy, a treaty was signed providing for the establishment of trade within the limits of Shimoda and Hakodate, and for the arrival of an American diplomat who would reside in Japan and arrange further agreements between the two countries.

The Americans were a revelation to the Japanese. For more than two centuries the rulers of Japan had maintained their country's isolation. Christians had been massacred, traders ousted, foreign books burned. The Japanese had known nothing of what went on beyond their watery walls. Now, at last, they were to find out.

The first meeting after the enclosed centuries was, on the surface at least, a great success. The Americans were astonishingly modern in their approach to the traditional Japanese representatives. They entertained the dignified Japanese gentlemen with music, performed by a gay black minstrel show. Louis Armstrong today is less surprising in his concerts abroad than were those early singers and performers of ragtime music and dance capers. The Japanese, it seems, were highly diverted and responded, then as now, with lovely geisha and overweight wrestlers. Champagne and sake were mutually enjoyed. Perry was delighted and all seemed well. He left, and other Americans soon followed.

For the first time the people of Japan were seeing a people altogether different from themselves. True, individual Japanese had visited China and Korea through the centuries, and had returned with news of other countries. But these were Asian countries and culturally related to the people in Japan. Americans were totally different. They were of many colors, their eyes blue, gray, brown, their hair yellow, red, black, straight or curly. In stature they varied greatly. They seemed to have no traditional culture, no set pattern of living. Their individual freedom seemed unlimited. Above all, they brought unique gifts throughout those early days and years of getting acquainted. Weapons hitherto unknown to the people of Japan were presented by the Americans—pistols, rifles, guns of every kind, even cannon were received with interest. Telegrams and telegraphic equipment, cameras, musical instruments were all new. Accustomed to sake, it was exciting, too, for the Japanese to discover wines, whiskey and liquors. They admired the freedom of Western men's dress, and especially the gaudy gold of military uniforms. The gift they welcomed above all was a railway, miniature but complete with engine and passenger cars. The Japanese had their first chance at a train ride. They were delighted. In a few decades railways spread all over Japan, a notable engineering accomplishment because of the mountainous terrain. The Japanese pleasure in locomotion still persists, and modern Japanese trains and railway services are among the best in the world.

All this took time, of course. In the beginning, in spite of their enchantment with the miniature train and other things, the Japanese people looked with distrust upon the Americans bearing gifts. Even after Perry's departure, second thoughts had already come to the people of Japan. They remembered a certain lack of restraint in the behavior of the Americans. Had this signified lack of respect for Japan? If so, the treaty could bring no good to the people. If on the other hand it was only exuberance in the Americans, it might mean that the Americans had gained too much from the treaty and were overjoyed. This, too, would be unfortunate for the people of Japan. Unable to decide the dilemma, a reaction set in, deepened by the fact that no sooner had other Western powers discovered the success of the Americans than they demanded like advantages. Accustomed to doing away with visitors they did not enjoy, the Japanese attacked foreigners who annoyed them. Retaliation was prompt. In addition to all else, it now became necessary to strengthen Japanese defense by modernization.

Thus did the coming of the Americans change the lives of the people of Japan. Not all of them were pleased by any means. The old men, especially, longed to return to the days of isolation and peace. Alas, it was too late! The people had grown used to excitement and diversion. They wanted to know more, not less, about the foreigners. A kind of illustrated newspaper came into existence, almost like our American cartoons, and this pictorial journalism became immensely popular.

In the midst of the struggle between the reactionaries who wished to restore Japan to its traditional cultural isolation and those who wanted modernization, American diplomat Townsend Harris suffered much. His efforts to obtain agreements with the Tokugawa shogunate met with continual frustration. Delay followed delay, and excuse upon excuse. Then, at last, events turned in Harris' favor, and on July 29, 1858, he was able to conclude a treaty which opened many Japanese ports to foreigners, maintained diplomatic and consular privileges, and allowed Americans the special right to be judged not by Japanese laws but by their own. Thus, after centuries of resistance, the Japanese had not only succumbed to the blandishments of foreigners but had accepted the troublesome provision known as extraterritoriality.

The ports of Yokohama, Nagasaki and Hakodate began active trade, and a Japanese embassy was established in the United States. Treaties were signed with other foreign nations and embassies established in each. The people of Japan, forced into the modern age by American invasion, were now open to the world. It was too much, too fast. In 1867 the Tokugawa shogunate fell and political power was returned to the Imperial Throne. The age of the Meiji had arrived.

It was the age of transition, the age of adjustment, but it began with the cry of the reactionaries: "Restore the Emperor and expel the Barbarian!" The Barbarian was still primarily the American—but he had succeeded better than he knew. More than ports and trade had been opened to the Western, the modern, world. Eyes, minds, had been opened. The daimyo, the feudal lords who had led the revolt against the hereditary shogunate, had thought that the rule of the people of Japan was theirs and the samurai, the "two-sword men," were their upholders. But the Meiji emperor followed a course of his own. Through a series of powerful reforms, by 1876 both daimyo and samurai had lost their feudal rights and were suspended from the government. The power of Buddhism was destroyed, and Shinto, the code of loyalty and obedience to the imperial house, came back into its own.

The reforms were made too swiftly to be welcomed even by the people. But rebels against the Meiji were promptly put down and, in spite of objection, the Meiji government went relentlessly on its way toward modernization, the whole purpose of which was to make of Japan a nation to be reckoned with in the modern world. The shogun were soon eliminated, and rule was direct under the throne. In 1889 the emperor gave his people a constitution. It defined the place of the people in the state, and it was written only after careful study of the constitutions of Western nations. Here again Japan exercised her genius for adaptation without mimicry. Prince Ito, who framed the constitution for the people of Japan, did so only after consultation, through Marquis Kido, with Herbert Spencer in England. He asked of this great English philosopher his opinion on the difficulties that Japan faced and how they might best be met. Spencer replied that the Japanese people had a bulwark of strength in their traditional obligation to their superiors. Under this secure leadership, Spencer said, the people could progress without danger of disruption from individualistic personalities.

Such judgment pleased the Meiji statesmen and they proceeded to define and stabilize "the advantages of observing proper station" between state and people, each having its own duties and the whole depending upon strong rule from above, ignoring public opinions. In this way Japan can be said to have modernized along the lines of her own traditions and culture. There was no such thing as an election; until 1940 the top governmental hierarchy was made up of those who could approach the emperor, those who were his closest advisers, and those who held such high office that their appointments bore the privy seal.

This is not to say, however, that the people of Japan during this period had no self-rule. The hamlets, villages and cities had, and still have, their own administrators to decide upon matters concerning the welfare of their people. These local administrations served to stabilize Japanese society, and to an extent have democratized it, in spite of the traditional imperial rule.

The Japanese constitution, though limited, was based upon law and mutual obligation between state and citizen, and it brought Japan new status in the modern world. At the same time the emperor and his able advisers, men who wanted to use the best scientific ideas of the West but to combine them with the ethics of the East, set about revitalizing Japan. With the aim of making a modern nation, the Japanese people faithfully followed the leadership of their government, the individual still in the ancient relationship to authority from above. Their progress was as amazing as that of the American people who were creating a nation out of a wilderness. The Japanese government ruled with full consideration for every level of society. The most modern techniques in transportation, in defense, in industry and agriculture, were established, and education in modernized schools was made compulsory. Ninety-eight per cent of the children were in school by the end of the Meiji period, a percentage considerably higher than that in the United States.

It was natural, with so practical-minded a government, that industry should have an important place in this remarkable advance. Industrial progress was necessary indeed, for agricultural land in Japan is limited, in spite of the beautifully terraced hills. Population was rising and too many people were on the land. Industry was the only answer, and under the direction of the government, industries sprang up throughout the nation. Soon the Japanese were able, through industrial fairs, to show the world that they were truly a modern people.

Two wars in the following decade established Japan as a military power. The first was the war with China over Korea. Japan coveted influence in, if not actual possession of, Korea, and she resented China's traditional suzerainty over the Korean people. In 1894 Japan sank a Chinese troopship and thus formally opened war. She swiftly seized the peninsula of Liaotung and then the harbor of Port Arthur. But France, Germany and Russia protested so vigorously that Japan was compelled to yield both her gains. The Japanese people were resentful, especially as during the next years these same countries proceeded to seize the same land, and more, for themselves. France took Kwangchow in south China, while Russia seized not only Port Arthur and Liaotung but the famous Tsingtao and Kiaochow ports.

In anger Japan watched Russian influence growing in coveted Korea, while her own trade area declined. When Russia demanded a neutral zone above the thirty-ninth parallel in Korea and complete control over the trade and resources of south Manchuria, Japan could no longer endure the threat of Russian expansionism. She broke off diplomatic relations with Russia and immediately attacked some of the

Russian navy ships in Port Arthur, declaring war the very next day. For eighteen months the Japanese fought the Russians bravely, always winning, to the admiration of President Theodore Roosevelt. Then, unable to bear the heavy cost of the war, Japan asked the President to mediate for peace. The Treaty of Portsmouth brought the war to an end. Russia was defeated, and the people of Japan were exhausted but triumphant.

In 1912 their beloved emperor died and the nation went into mourning. His had been a brilliant reign, and his hold upon the people remained firm. In sixty short years the people of Japan had been welded into a strong modern nation. Five great universities had been opened, and young men were educated into the world of science, arts and letters, while in turn they carried to the world the influences of Japanese architecture, art and industry. The people of Japan in a little more than half a century had been transformed from feudal isolation into a great world power. It was a feat as remarkable, I repeat, as that of the American people in building a nation out of a wilderness. They shared the same spirit, the same inspiration, these two peoples, and in some ways are much alike.

How then could it come about that during those years we, Japanese and Americans, became enemies? They were the years of estrangement, those years. During them we drew apart, each people engrossed in its own growth, each too busy to reach a hand to the other. Then there was the difficulty of communication. Neither people learns a foreign language easily. Americans feel no need to learn, in the vastness of our territory; and the Japanese have no need because of their geographical isolation. There were ideals and concepts, too, that our two peoples did not share, and an almost total lack of meaningful contact on a personal level. The Americans and the Japanese had not taken time to know or understand each other.

IV

IN THOSE DAYS of our historic separation I was myself part of Asia. American by ancestry and birth, my life had been spent almost entirely in China, and it was from China that I watched the changing Japanese, and shared the Chinese consternation at what was taking place. For the impetus given by the energy of the Meiji continued into the twentieth century and the new leaders of Japan were dreaming again the dreams of Hideyoshi in the sixteenth century when he had asked permission of the emperor to sally forth and conquer China. This we knew very well, we who lived in China. We knew, too, that Japan was land hungry and, moreover, that she had a natural and increasing fear of encroaching Western colonialism. The people of Japan would never accept colonial rule, that we knew.

Alas, China was in a period of weakness. Since revolutionists had destroyed the throne, no new dynasty was possible and the people were without the leadership of government. It was the ideal time for Japanese dreamers to dream again. Even the West had helped them, for in the First World War Japan had sided with the Allies. Her sole contribution to the Allied cause, however, as I have said, had been the occupation of areas in China that had been seized previously by Germany. When the war ended, Japan did not return these areas to China but remained firmly entrenched upon Chinese soil. She became even more entrenched as time went on, for in the national confusion of a China with no central government, various contenders for central rule, or warlords, as we called them, fought one another in local areas. These contending warlords, whom the revolutionary Chiang Kai-shek was trying to eliminate, were always short of funds to maintain their vast armies and their households crowded with concubines and children, and they were continually borrowing huge sums of money from the willing Japanese military leaders, giving in collateral Chinese mines, railways, and even land concessions. Since these warlords were never able to pay their debts, China was falling into Japanese hands bit by bit.

In the midst of all this, Communism had added its confusion. Chiang Kai-shek had forsaken its circle and was endeavoring to renew old forces and assume leadership, when Japan struck. I remember the day, the very hour, when I heard the news. The year was 1931. I was waiting in my study in my home in Nanking, China, for Mr. Lung, the old Chinese scholar who was my consultant while I was translating the ancient Chinese classic, a novel entitled *Shui Hu Chuan*. He was late, and this surprised me for he was always prompt. When he arrived he looked pale. I rose as usual, in common courtesy to a scholar, but he did not seem to notice. He sat down and, drawing his fan from the collar of his robe where he always carried it, he began to fan himself in agitation.

"Has Tai-tai seen the wall newspapers today?" he demanded in Chinese, for he spoke no English. Being a gentleman, he never addressed me directly but always by the high honorific of a married lady.

"This humble one has not left the house today on account of being too busy," I replied with responding courtesy.

His face became more agitated. "The Japanese have seized Manchuria," he said.

We stared at each other in mutual consternation, the future equally clear to both. There would be war. But who would fight it? China was torn by revolution and Communism. Chiang Kai-shek, having renounced Communism, was struggling for a foothold as the next ruler and was not ready to wage a foreign war.

"Will your country fight for us?" His voice was a whisper.

"No," I said. "My people won't understand. They are too far away."

"Then," he said, "there will be another world war."

It was difficult to work that day on the ancient novel, and yet it was strangely significant, for the old book was a tangled tale of revolution and angry men. We worked only half the usual afternoon, I remember, for Mr. Lung's mind was in distress and mine was distracted by what I foresaw in the future. If there were a world war I would have to leave China and go to my own country. I could see the world dividing between two dark forces, one in Europe, one in Russia. It was not difficult to know with which side Japan would ally herself. Her military leaders had been trained in Germany.

In the difficult days that followed, the days that mounted into months and years, events took their invincible way. Japan was with us night and day with new encroachments. I thought of the Japanese people I knew so well and had always loved. Did they realize what was happening to them as well as to us? Did they know what dangerous dreams their leaders were having? Some day they would be fighting not only the Chinese but my own people, the Americans. Did they know?

For in the somber march of those days it became obvious to me that when Japanese military leaders attacked the Chinese it would be carefully planned to coincide with a war in Europe, in which England and all European nations would be involved. In this case America would be compelled to side with her former allies and, with us thus engaged, Japan would be free to do as she pleased in China. Indeed, she was already doing as she pleased, while Chiang Kai-shek was desperately trying to unify the country under the new Nationalist government.

Those were the days when any fantasy could become a reality, and we woke one morning to discover that Chiang had been kidnaped by the Communists when he went to confer with the young Marshal of Manchuria, who was a political refugee of considerable stature and not to be ignored. With the accusation that he was not willing to fight Japan, Chiang was forced to compromise and join his Communist enemies in such a war. It was then that I began to pack trunks and arrange my household for a long absence. I hoped it would not be forever, but I knew it would be, if through war and consequent victory, Communism came into power in China.

I remember well the long sea voyage across the Pacific, for air travel over that vast watery space was still an idea and not reality. I lingered in Japan, leaving the ship each time we were in port, in Nagasaki, Kobe and Yokohama. I walked the streets, I sat in parks, everywhere I watched the people, pain in my foreboding heart. Would the day come when we must be enemies? If so, they showed no signs of it. They were calm and courteous, always busy and, it seemed to me, content.

It was in Kobe that I spent a happy day, which afterwards I

commemorated in a book for children entitled *One Bright Day*. Exactly as it happened, I wrote it down. The ship docked early in the morning. My two little daughters were restless from the sea voyage, their father was busy, and so I decided to take them ashore alone for the day. It would be a long noisy day aboard ship, for we were refueling for the rest of the journey and we would not sail until sunset. I planned some hours in a park near the dock, and thither we went, the three of us on foot.

I had scarcely settled myself on a bench, the little girls playing on the grass, when an old gentleman, a Japanese in dignified dark silk robes, drove past in a horse-drawn carriage. When he saw us he called to his coachman and the carriage stopped. Descending, the old gentleman approached me, and in good English inquired if he could be of service to me. I thanked him and explained my circumstances, whereupon he explained in turn.

"Madam, I am taking some leisure today because of my health. You are here only for the day. Let me make it pleasant for you and your children by showing you our city."

Something like this he said, and instinctively I trusted him, stranger that he was. I thanked him, called the children, and we got into the carriage. All during the morning of that bright day we drove about the city and its environs. When noon came he returned us safely to the ship and I thought he would say goodbye. But no, since the ship would not sail until evening, he proposed that we take the children to a beach where they and I could enjoy a swim, since the afternoon was very warm.

I accepted, somewhat surprised that I did, and in an hour he returned in the carriage and we drove several miles to a fine beach, crowded with Japanese families. The dressing rooms were clean, bathing suits could be rented, and we prepared ourselves, the children and I. The old gentleman said that he could not go into the sea, for the cold water did not suit his age, but he would sit on the beach and take care of our clothes and my handbag. I had a moment of prudence. Passport, money, and travel tickets were in the handbag. I did not really know the old gentleman, charming as he was. But I had gone too far now for distrust. The children were pulling me toward the sea. I yielded, and we joined the throng of people. The sky was blue, the sun was hot, the water clear and refreshing. Now and again I glanced toward the shore. There the old gentleman sat cross-legged on the sand.

I forgot him in the pure pleasure of the sea. Barely in time we ran, wet and laughing, to dress ourselves and climb into the carriage again. The old gentleman handed me my bag and its valuables and we went back to the ship. The gangway was waiting and we rushed aboard, waving to the erect old figure on the dock. He stood there motionless and waiting until the ship eased away. Is it any wonder that I called my little book *One Bright Day*?

It remained thus in my memory during all the dark days that were to come, the days of war and enmity. On that dreadful day when bombs fell on Pearl Harbor I recalled that other day when a gentle old man in Japan, a Japanese, left his imprint forever upon me and my children, a memory of kindness to a stranger, and I knew the day would come when our two peoples must be friends again. But the day was long in coming, and many died on both sides of the sea we share.

While I write these words I am reminded of people in my own country, who were also people of Japan, although some of them were American citizens. Many of their sons were loyal American soldiers who fought bravely for our cause in Europe, mainly in Italy, where many of them died in bitter warfare. Yet in the exigencies of war, other people of Japan upon our soil were compelled to leave their homes, gardens and fields and go into our western deserts to live in barracks, under military guards. Yet even there, one characteristic of the Japanese shone forth clearly. It was their love of beauty.

Without beauty the Japanese cannot live. If it be in a desert, they create gardens of sand and rock, and out of dried roots and leafless branches they carve figures of soaring birds and waterfowl. In the strange wilderness of the American west they remained themselves, changing never but adapting to the change. Out of the desert they created gardens and out of the bare shacks in which they were housed they created beauty. I have a photograph of the twisted branch of some desert plant, but imaginative Japanese eyes saw in it the shape of a stately heron and so created it. I longed to possess the beauty for my own, but the creator could not part with it and gave me instead the picture.

"As long as I live," he told me, "I cannot part with that heron. It is a symbol to me of the day I came out of the desert of despair. Beauty had fled. The harsh sun beat down upon the harsh sand. The wooden barracks offered no escape from the heat. I thought I must die because there was no beauty left in my life. Then I saw this branch, a dead thing, but it took on the shape of life. I took it in my hands. With a small kitchen knife for a tool, I freed the shape and in so doing I discovered that beauty is everywhere."

"BEAUTY IS EVERYWHERE." It is everywhere in Japan, and wherever there are Japanese. Love for beauty is fundamental to the Japanese nature.

Isolation led to estrangement, and estrangement became war. Yet Japan's long periods of deliberate seclusion were not altogether evil. They provided time for the Japanese to ponder their own ways, to solidify their own customs, to develop their own matchless art. They were, of course, profoundly influenced by the nature and setting of their beautiful islands. Beauty pervaded every area of their lives. The simplest and poorest household in Japan came to have its place of beauty, an alcove in which a scroll was hung, with a vase beneath containing perhaps a single simple flower. Today's Japanese home still has that alcove, flower, and scroll. Houses are kept scrupulously neat and clean. There are slums, of course, in the great cities; there are also untidy housewives, but of these there are few. The Japanese house does not lend itself to disorder. A room is used for many purposes, a living room or study or library or guest room by day, a bedroom by night when the mattress and quilt are removed from their storage place in the closet. Floors are kept immaculate by deep resilient mats, and shoes are taken off at the entrance to the house. Furniture is almost nonexistent, a low table or desk, some cushions, a bookshelf perhaps, and that is all. There is nothing with which to create disorder. Walls are sliding screens and a room may be made large or small by adjusting them. One wall, in almost every Japanese house, slides open to reveal a tiny but exquisite garden that is an extension of the house. In a room there is one scroll in the alcove called the tokonoma, not two scrolls or an oversized painting. There is a slim spray of flowers, or perhaps a slender branch, not a great vase crammed with cut stalks and full-blown blossoms. Nature is worshiped, but it has been tamed. The beauty of Japan is a disciplined beauty, reflecting a disciplined people—disciplined and determined. Japanese poetry is contained in brief verses, Japanese drama is stylized, almost ritual.

This is the Japan I have known all my life, these are her people.

WHAT CHANGES have taken place since the war? The most shattering event in the entire history of the Japanese people has been her experience with the American people, first in her hopeless vanquishment and second in the American occupation. Until World War II Japan had always been successful, achieving a formidable series of victories as a result of her military adventures. Add to this her amazing progress in all aspects of modern life, add to this the characteristic self-confidence and self-assurance of any island people not in the close proximities of continental peoples, and it was perhaps inevitable that Japanese leaders felt ready to assume control over Asia, at least. That the leaders led their people to disastrous defeat instead of the glorious victory so ebulliently prophesied shook the Japanese to their very depths. They were accustomed to earthquakes which destroyed their homes and the land upon which they stood, but this defeat in war was more than bombed cities and thousands dead. It was a defeat of their entire being, mind and heart as well as body. They were no longer the people they thought they were, had always thought they were. They were faced with an unknown people, themselves, and in an unknown world. The shadow of colonization had never darkened their lives; among all Asian countries, they alone had remained independent and free. The same isolation that had allowed them to develop in their own way had blinded them to the great progress being made in the rest of the world and had given them an unreal picture of themselves, an exaggerated idea of their strength and international stature.

Among all Asian peoples the Japanese were the ones who naturally least understood the Western peoples. For though they had been inquisitive and eager to learn from other countries, it had always been on their own terms. In spite of the progressive Japanese spirit and curiosity, Japanese persons visiting the West had carried their insularity with them. They did not go abroad with empty minds, to learn for the sake of knowledge. They went to find what would be useful to Japan. This attitude prevented them from making any true evaluation of Western peoples. It prevented them from understanding the world.

When defeated, they were therefore a lost people, confounded and confused, their leaders mistaken and untrustworthy, their emperor no longer deified, even their gods no longer valid. Suddenly they found themselves stripped of pretensions and spiritual support. They were exposed, vulnerable, totally bewildered. And they were to be occupied by an unknown people, Americans, a people as ignorant of the Japanese as the Japanese were ignorant of them.

With the end of the war the most difficult task of all confronted the people of Japan and the United States. We had been enemies and now, somehow, we must be friends. The people of Japan had been all but destroyed by our attacks. Tokyo lay in ruins, as did many another city. Kyoto alone of the most famous cities stood unharmed. It is a city singularly lovely, rich in tradition and ancient monuments, and the American government had decreed that it should be spared. Little else was untouched, and the bombing culminated in the fateful dropping of the atomic bombs on Hiroshima and Nagasaki.

In the dread silence that followed, two proud peoples faced each other as strangers, one the conqueror, the other the conquered. Neither side was prepared for what took place.

The Japanese people expected the worst. Their military leaders had warned them that occupation would be cruel and total, that Americans were brutal and savage. Again the people of Japan found their leaders wrong. The Americans were neither brutal nor savage. Individual men committed brutal and savage acts occasionally, but they were punished by their own officers. Americans, in their turn, did not know what to expect of a people who had fought with such suicidal dedication, and they were wary. They, too, found that they had braced themselves unnecessarily. The Japanese were surprised by the kindness and consideration of the victors and the Americans were surprised by the dignity and courtesy of the vanquished.

Yes, the postwar period has brought us face to face with the people of Japan. We had passed through years of more than total separation. Before Pearl Harbor we had been strangers. After Pearl Harbor we were enemies. People to people, we could not meet. Face to face, we met only in mortal combat in the jungles of Asia and the islands of the Pacific. Hate and fear distorted American and Japanese faces alike and propaganda fed our mutual fury. Communication was impossible until combat ceased.

As strangers in the silence after war we met again, this time upon Japanese soil. Victors and vanquished, we still could not communicate. We were compelled to wait until we discovered each other in the necessity of living together. Both sides are to be commended for the mood in which we undertook the new and difficult life of the occupation. Under the wise leadership of General Douglas MacArthur, the American approach was one of firmness combined with a sincere consideration of Japanese feelings. The over-all policies of the American government were followed with brilliance by General MacArthur. The basic decision was to place the responsibility upon the Japanese people themselves for the administration and reconstruction of their own country. This decision was in contrast to the policies carried out in Germany and Italy, and it showed a perceptive understanding of the capacity and maturity of the Japanese people, and of their unshaken national unity, maintained through many centuries. General MacArthur fulfilled his mission, above all, without disturbing the structure of the Japanese government. He addressed his communications directly to the imperial government, setting forth the goals which the Japanese were to achieve. If a particular Japanese minister felt he could not reach the assigned goal, he could resign and be replaced, or he could plead his case, and the directive might be eased. Good will on both sides was the result of such enlightened policy. Lacking good will, the people of Japan might have been sullen and uncooperative, their pride mortified. As it was, they worked with sincerity to achieve the goals set forth, and without rancor.

It is characteristic of the Japanese people to accept fate without rebellion, when convinced that it *is* fate, and to learn from their own mistakes. Thus in the nineteenth century when it had become obvious that their ancient isolation could no longer be maintained in the face of a changing world, they had moved swiftly and firmly into the reforms of the Meiji period. In the same way they accepted defeat when the atomic bomb was twice used, and resolved to use the defeat as a lesson for achieving their next goal: that of a new and peaceful golden age for Japan, and even for the world. Their greatness is proved by their ability to acknowledge defeat as evidence of their own mistake in judgment and to proceed therefrom to constructive action.

That they are able to exhibit such self-discipline I attribute to their unshaken national unity, based upon the structure of their government. The Japanese people can change direction with speed and thoroughness when they become convinced that change is essential. They have been and are rebels but not revolutionists. Rebels demand progress, but revolutionists demand destruction. Within the firm structure of Japanese society rebels are constant and effective, but no one wants revolution. The American policy makers wisely understood the importance of maintaining the structure, and within its security many changes were effected in Japanese society. This was possible, too, because the people of Japan were not humiliated in their defeat. Had they been compelled to suffer humiliation they undoubtedly would have taken the revenge half expected by the Americans. As it was, the attitudes of those in power permeated to the smallest village, and American men were amazed at the friendliness of a people who only weeks—nay, days—before had been their enemies.

The American occupation was humane, considerate and constructive beyond any known in history. Had the Japanese been a people less noble they might have taken advantage of this. But they are a noble people, able to accept what is offered in good spirit. There were mistakes on both sides, quickly recognized and mended. The ancient habits of Japanese courtesy held; American good will responded. The enmity that had started so early to fade soon vanished altogether and an extraordinary mutual friendliness took its place. The two peoples discovered each other for the first time as they really were and came to a new understanding each of the other. The mutual discovery grew into a genuine liking which in many individual cases was expressed in love. Americans were married to Japanese women, children were born, sometimes out of wedlock, and thus the two races mingled.

Both peoples have been influenced in many ways, each by the other. The two cultures have remained separate, it is true, but there is scarcely an area which has not changed, East to accommodate West, and West to accommodate East. It is not too much to say that the American people are more influenced today by the Japanese than by any other people. Americans have discovered that they can understand, admire and even like an Asian people, and the Japanese, if I am not mistaken, have a like feeling toward the Americans.

The influence goes beyond this, however. Japanese life has been profoundly changed by the experience of war, by occupation, and by close contact with Americans. Their dress, their food, their houses, their amusements, their entire economic life, all have been and are still changing. But the most profound change that I have observed between the old Japan and the new is in the people.

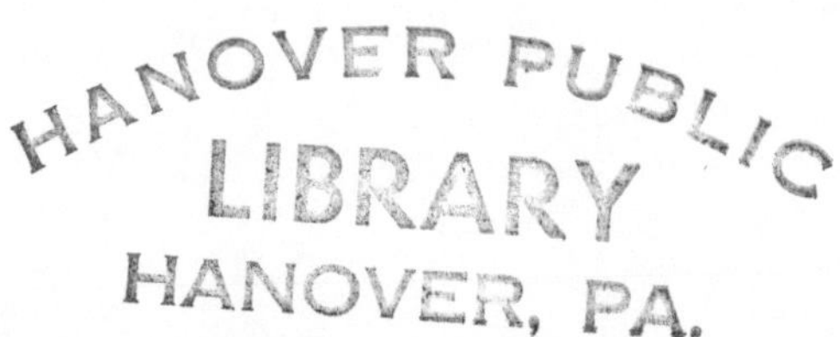

V

AS I HAVE SAID, Japan has been a part of my life and experience since early childhood. Instead of New York, Chicago, San Francisco and other American cities, I knew Tokyo, Yokohama, Osaka, Kyoto, Nagasaki. I lived in various places, visited in many more, had Japanese friends and acquaintances, and was at home in Japan only slightly less than in China. I was therefore not prepared for the postwar Japanese, and it took me some time to discover the depth and variety of change.

Such change usually takes a long time and may even take centuries, but in Japan it is sharply defined. However modern she was before the war and consequent occupation, she was still the old Japan. After the occupation she was the new

Japan, and I had to seek out the old. In most countries change begins at the periphery. People travel and bring back new ways and ideas. The center is the last point to feel the new. In Japan the opposite has been true. As long as the center of government did not change, the Japanese people did not change. However widely individuals might have traveled, however many were the new ideas and objects they brought back, Japan did not change so long as the emperor remained the divine center of life, a symbol of the people, a deity, descendant of the sun-goddess. It must be said that General MacArthur and the American government showed great understanding of the Japanese people and their heritage when they decided that the emperor was not to be removed even though he was no longer to be regarded as a deity.

At war's end, Japanese soldiers had been stirred to their utmost by the decree of the emperor, for without him there could be no Japan. He was above criticism, a figure remote and lofty whom none could approach, unchanging, inviolable. When the emperor decreed, the war stopped. Before the emperor went on the radio to announce surrender, there had been Japanese military men who tried to prevent it and even threw a cordon about the palace. Once he had spoken, however, he was obeyed. That is why, when American troops landed on Japanese airfields, they were treated courteously. The emperor had decreed change, and there was change.

Yet there was no change. After all I have said about change, I repeat: There was no change. That is to say there was no change at the heart, which is the emperor. All that is new in Japan is new at his command and therefore not new. So long as the center remains unchanged, Japan will to the same extent be unchanged. Whether the externals, the modern techniques, the new exposures, will penetrate to the heart is a question to ponder, but only time can give the answer. Until and unless it does, we must realize that in all the change in Japanese life today, there is still the changeless and the unchangeable. The hard core is there, yesterday, today, and, so far as one can see now, forever.

Where then is the change? Well, everyday things have changed. The very atmosphere of the country is changed. There is much less formality than there used to be. People still bow but not as deeply. They are not so frank as to be rude, but they are much more frank than ever they were before Americans arrived en masse on their shores. They sit more easily on chairs instead of cushions, with the result that in the younger generation legs are longer. They eat more meat and less rice and they are healthier for it and more gay. The old delicate, wistful melancholy, so native to the Japanese character, is not entirely gone, but nearly so. People still commit suicide, but not so easily as they once did and often for less romantic or traditional reasons. Crowds are more cheerful, children more lively. One hears laughter.

I perceived the change immediately, but it took a little time to discover where it focused. I decided at last that it began with and in women. Nothing and no one in Japan has changed as much as the women. When I remember the withdrawn, silent, subdued women I once knew in Japan, and when I see the brisk, competent, outgoing women now, I am amazed.

This new Japanese woman somehow manages to please by the very traits she used once to conceal. She has forsaken her formalities, her studied grace, her disciplined silence. She is frank, often joyous, and she will speak up where once she would have pretended to agree. Yet she knows when to yield. I think of my competent little Japanese secretary, a young and pretty woman who was educated in a modern school. Learning that Japanese men still consider it their right to visit bars after work hours, these bars being a sort of substitute for old-fashioned geisha houses, I asked Haruko if she put up with this habit in her husband.

"Oh yes," she said calmly.

"But does he come home at two o'clock in the morning?" I asked.

"Oh yes," she said again.

"And you wait up for him?"

"Oh yes," she said.

I remonstrated. "Come now—without complaints?"

She gave me a sidewise, woman's look. "At first I did complain. I cried."

"And he?"

"Then he did not come home at all."

"So?"

"I stopped complaining and I do not cry now. I wait for him, I have hot tea ready."

The emperor in his palace, the man in the house, the center remains unchanged.

Nevertheless there is a new honesty within the woman of today's Japan. She does not hide or pretend. Few Japanese women ever pretended to the extent of falsifying their figures. Perhaps they did not need to, for one seldom sees a fat Japanese woman. Indeed I cannot remember ever having seen one. Japanese diet is simple, healthy and slimming. At any rate, the Japanese woman does not bind her waist or enlarge her bosom by artifices. Her breasts are usually small, she tends to have a boyish figure. Since Japanese men do not have the fanatical breast-fixation of Western men, they seem to like the home product. With the time and attention American women give to themselves, Japanese women could look much more exotic than they do, but they do not place so much emphasis on appearance. For instance, a young American man married to a Japanese wife said recently, "Several times I've given my wife money for a permanent wave. Instead she spends it for flowers, or something special for dinner!" And the young American does not object.

Another example of this lack of pretense is the case of a

young girl who was going to meet her husband for the first time at an acquaintance party. Though she wore glasses only part of the time, she wore them on this occasion.

"I want him to see me at my worst," she explained. She did marry the young man, and they are very happy, I am told.

Japanese men apparently are not as concerned as American men about how their wives look. More important to the Japanese man is how his wife fulfills her wifely duties. The result is that instead of one divorce in every five marriages, as in America, divorce in Japan takes place only once in twenty-five marriages, even though divorce is easier in Japan than in the United States, incompatibility being legitimate grounds. The "love" marriages are not so successful as the arranged ones. One in every ten of these marriages ends in divorce.

Marriage itself, however, remains strangely traditional. I took some pains to discover just how traditional when I was in Japan not long ago, for I had been disconcerted upon discovering how much like American teen-agers the Japanese teen-agers are nowadays. Today young couples stroll hand in hand through city streets, a thing unheard of in the past. Young people, boys and girls, gather for long hours in coffee shops, and roar noisily about town on motorcycles or scooters. Japanese "Beatles" are the rage. A friend in the motion picture industry took me to a huge rock-and-roll theater in Tokyo, and there I saw and heard a vast expanse crowded with Japanese teen-agers, mostly girls and nearly all of them dressed in skirts and middy blouses. On the stage were the singers, all boys except one, and all long-haired types, wailing out love songs in Japanese and English. One boy specialized in our western cowboy songs, which he sang quite well in English, although I was told he understood not one word of that language. The girls moaned and swayed to his music and screamed at appropriate moments. When a favorite singer finished a song, his special fans rushed to the stage to garland him.

Seeing all this and being suitably astonished, I supposed that marriage customs had altered and that love marriages, Western style, were now the fashion. I found I was wrong. Marriage in Japan continues to be a family affair. When these screaming girls and long-haired boys reach the proper age, the parents begin a search for suitable mates for them. Most marriages in Japan, I discovered, are still *miai,* or arranged, the theory being that love comes after marriage rather than before. Once a young man has a secure job, it is time for his parents to make their choice for him or, and this is more common these days, to present him with a list of carefully screened prospects from which to make his own selection. A go-between is chosen, whose task is to advise the family on the suitability of various available young girls and eventually to arrange a meeting of the prospective bride and groom. The girl and boy, it is true, may express their preferences to the go-between, and may even achieve a parentally approved love marriage if the choice has been made from the recommended list.

When likely candidates are found and offered, the two sets of parents carefully go over the situation, exchanging pictures, collecting family histories, comparing educational qualifications, health, temperaments, social status, wealth. Astrology is also important, in order that the years may be compared. A girl born in the Year of the Hare, for example, may be unruly. Nor should the number four be found anywhere, since it is an unlucky number, just as nineteen is an unlucky age. If all signs are favorable the go-between sets the time and place for the young couple to meet. If this first meeting, or *miai,* is a success, then engagement presents are exchanged and the wedding is arranged. A fortunate day is chosen, and a lucky month. Cherry blossoms fall in April and maple leaves in October, and these are therefore considered unlucky months for a wedding. November and December, however, are considered most auspicious. Of course many families in modern Japan do not believe in all this, but custom tends to follow tradition, nevertheless.

After the miai and the exchange of gifts, the young couple may meet again several times, usually at public places and in the presence of others, to get acquainted. Granted, they cannot get to know each other very well under the circumstances, but nevertheless here is the modern touch, for in the old days no such meetings could have taken place.

On her wedding day this modern girl of Japan, who when she is a teen-ager indulges in rock-and-roll and out of her teens becomes a smartly dressed office worker, reverts to the past. She rents a wig to make her look like an old-fashioned girl with a high coiffure, on top of which she wears a wide white headband which is supposed to hide the horns of jealousy, the cardinal sin for a wife. This is a reminder, even on her wedding day, that she is not to expect her husband to be faithful to her, nor is she to be jealous when the inevitable diversion of interest takes place. Her wig is held in place by tortoise-shell combs upon which are carved the characters for plum tree, fir and bamboo, each with its own significance of eternal loyalty, patience and beauty. Her costume is costly. It is the traditional kimono, sleeves almost to the floor, and the obi of such heavy silk brocade that it may use as much material as the kimono and cost hundreds of dollars. True, one may rent the costume, but purchase is considered socially more sound, though extravagant, for the costume may never be worn again.

After the ritual drinking of sake before the shrine of Shinto gods, a Shinto priest presiding, the white headband—almost a hat—is removed. It is usually made of white silk and somewhat hides the bride's face, especially as she keeps her head bowed. A naughty tradition has it that the purpose of this sort of headband was to keep the groom from seeing the bride's face, for once having caught a glimpse of ugliness, he might run away, never to return.

The wedding feast follows the marriage ceremony; there may be musical and theatrical entertainment and the usual joking and laughter which increase in bawdiness with the flow of sake. In the country regions and less modern cities, there is horseplay, and guests may force the couple into bed and peep through holes in the shoji to watch what follows. To avoid horseplay, young couples nowadays usually leave for a honeymoon elsewhere. This is the new Japan.

But—and here is the old again—whatever the wedding and wherever the honeymoon, there comes a moment when the two are alone. The man must now assert himself. He must speak to the woman in curt, lordly tones. She is not to think he is afraid of her or that he is weakened by love. Their separate roles must be made clear and distinct. She is the submissive one, he is in command. Never must she call him by his first name, nor omit the honorable title due to a husband from a wife. I have made a private research into this moment of clarification between husband and wife and apparently tradition has not changed. Except for those Japanese who are American born, each wife confessed to this important moment.

Is it possible, one may ask, that young people in Japan still accept the traditional marriage customs? Well, I have a young friend who was married several months ago, who saw his wife for the first time at the miai seven weeks before the wedding. The mother of his best friend was the go-between, and the miai at her house brought together not only the prospective bride and groom but their parents as well. Afterwards either young person could have called the whole thing off, but neither chose to. They had three dates—a movie, a concert, and a tour of the zoo. And then they were wed.

Unromantic? Perhaps. But I think the Japanese way has certain advantages over our own. In Japan one still gives great weight to the wisdom of one's elders when taking the most important step in life. As for my young friend, his marriage is working out well. He is already deeply attached to his new wife, a girl he had not so much as touched before their wedding day.

There has been some slight break with tradition, of course, for in the old days there was no question of choice. Son or daughter married the partner selected by the parents, and that was usually that. Today there has been an amalgamation of old tradition and modern custom, and I believe it is for the best. Even American friends of mine, men, have told me that they no longer think romantic reasons are the best reasons for marrying. The Asian way, they say, is much more sensible. Those who have come around to this way of thinking say that if a man marries on the advice of his parents, he will know that he is at least marrying a woman who matches him and his family, and that his parents probably can choose a better wife for him than he himself can. Now that tradition has relaxed to the extent of permitting choice from a group, both parents and offspring are satisfied. I am not sure that we in the West have made so much progress. Lin Yutang, the Chinese writer, said that the time a man is least able to decide his life is when he is in love, and thus he marries at the time when he is the greatest fool.

And I am reminded of another Japanese friend, no longer so very young but headstrong in his youth. He used to be one of the famous radio commentators in Japan, and a writer whose books have been published in the United States. As a young man he insisted that a love marriage was the proper thing. Having fallen in love, he rebelled against his family and the girl they chose for him, and he married the very independent young girl of his own choice. His parents were outraged and disowned him completely. The young couple lived in this country for a while and had four or five children together. I do not know whether he became more Japanese as he grew older, or whether he had always been more Japanese than he thought, but in spite of the children the marriage

The following color plates were engraved directly from original Anscochrome® color transparency films of General Aniline & Film Corporation with whose cooperation this section of *The People of Japan* was produced.

OPPOSITE

Schoolgirl. Oiso, Honshu.

Fishing boats off Hokkaido.

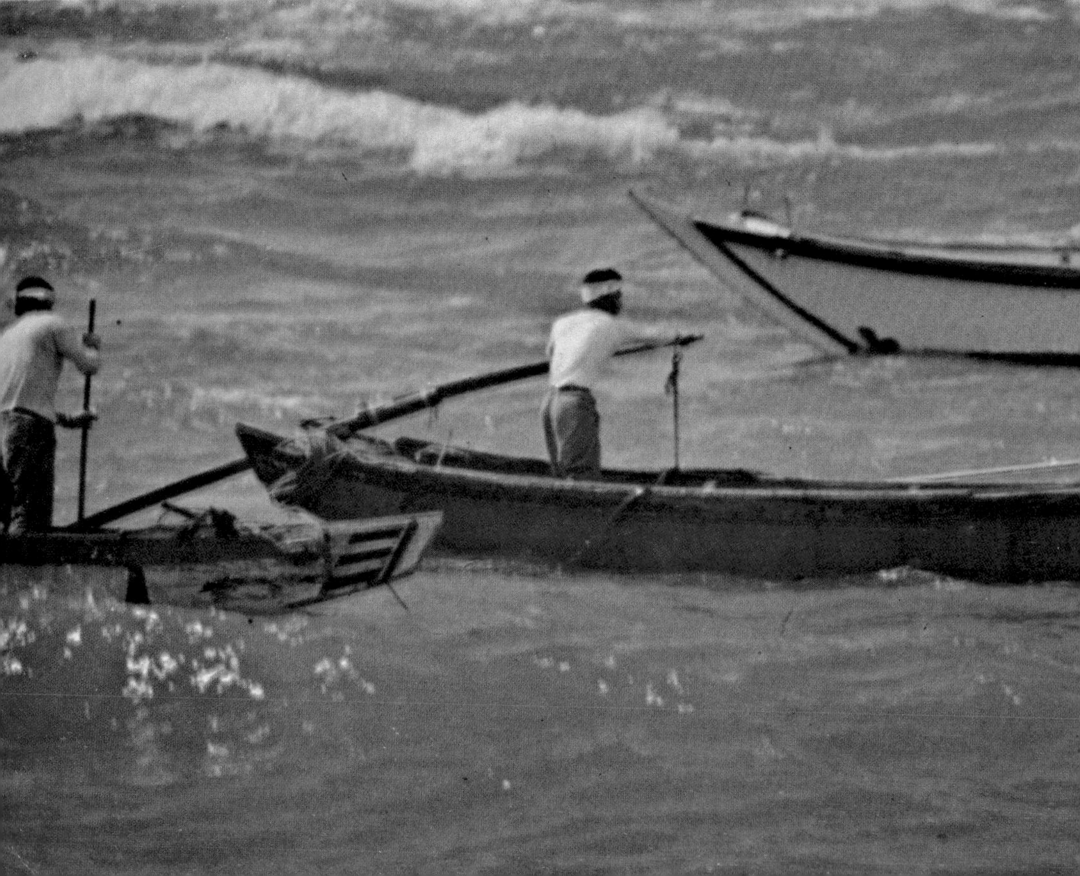

Workers in a steel plant. Sasebo, Kyushu.

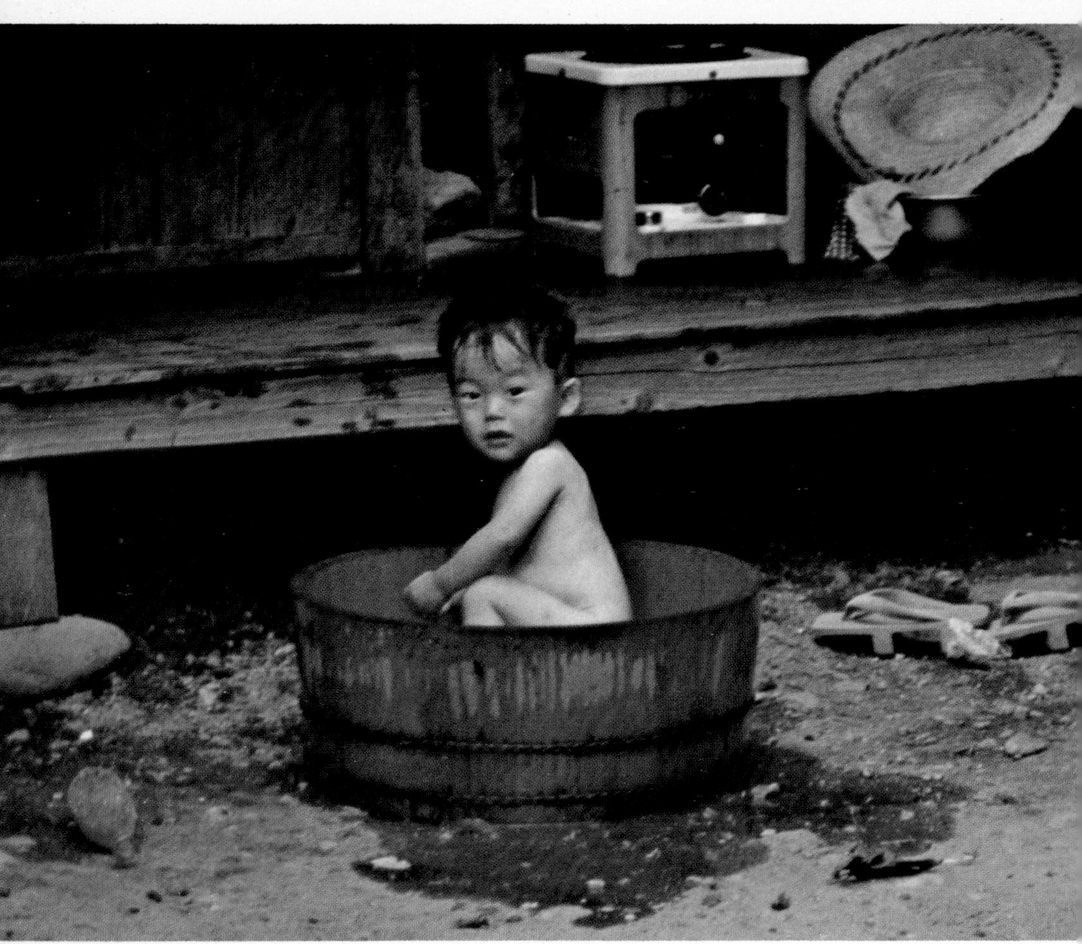

In a country village north of Nikko, Honshu.

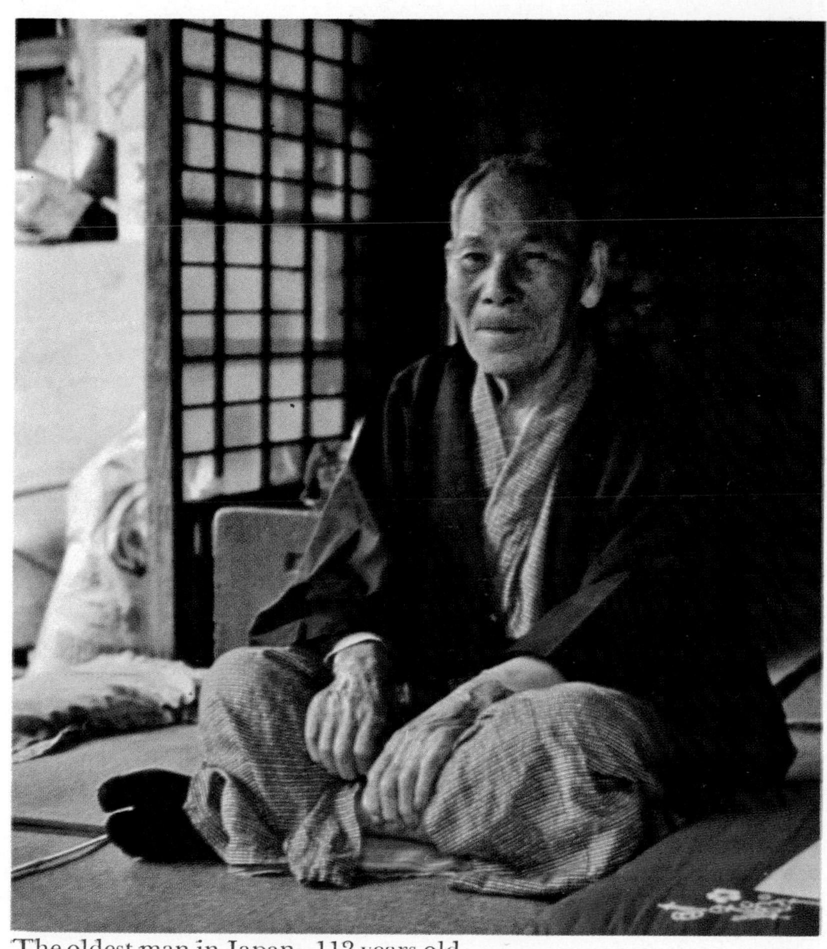

The oldest man in Japan—112 years old.

Children of Yokosuka.

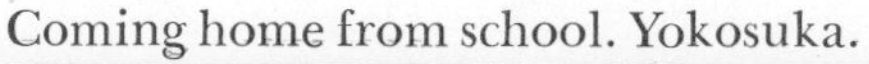

Coming home from school. Yokosuka.

Illuminated floats in the Samurai Festival. Aomori, Honshu.

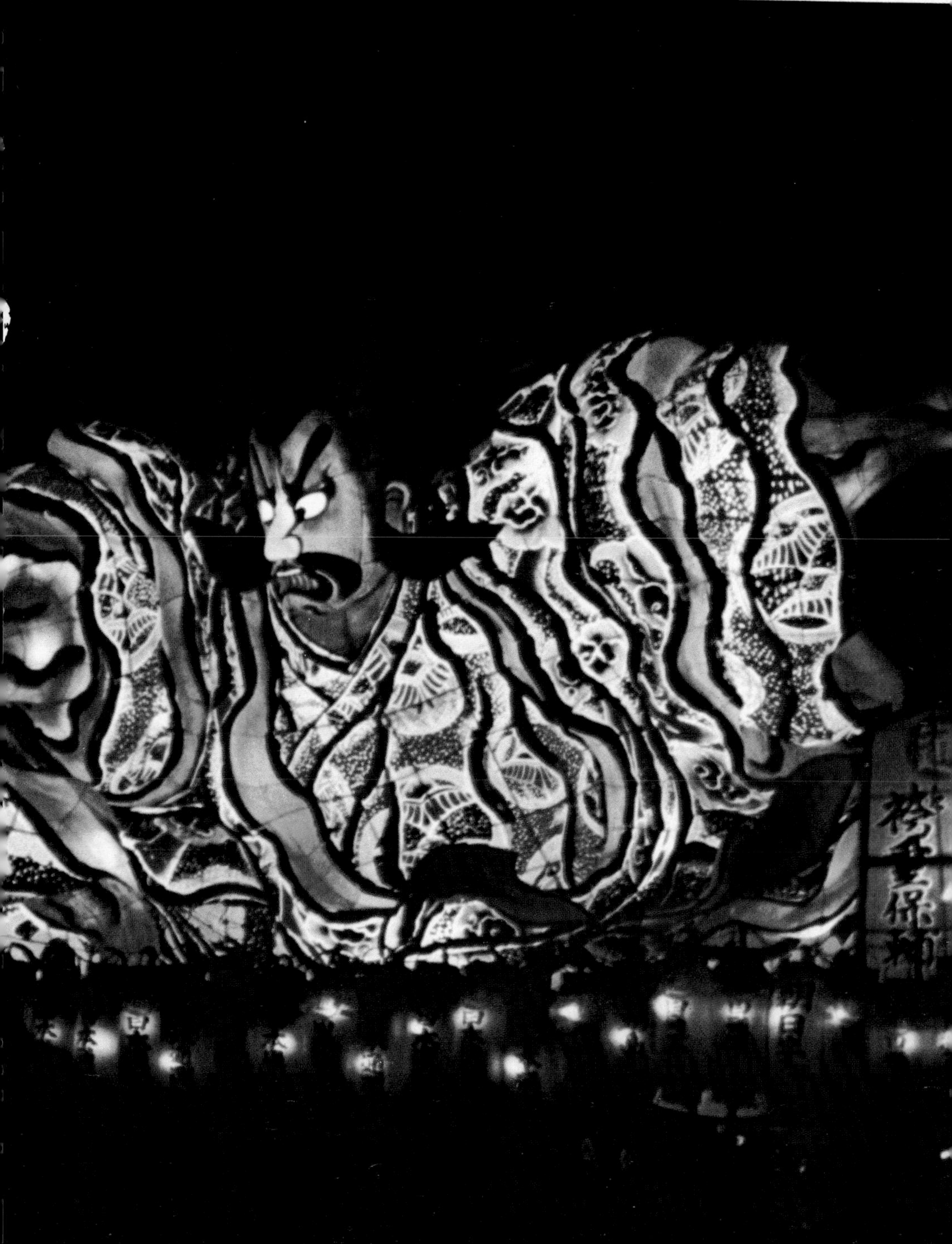

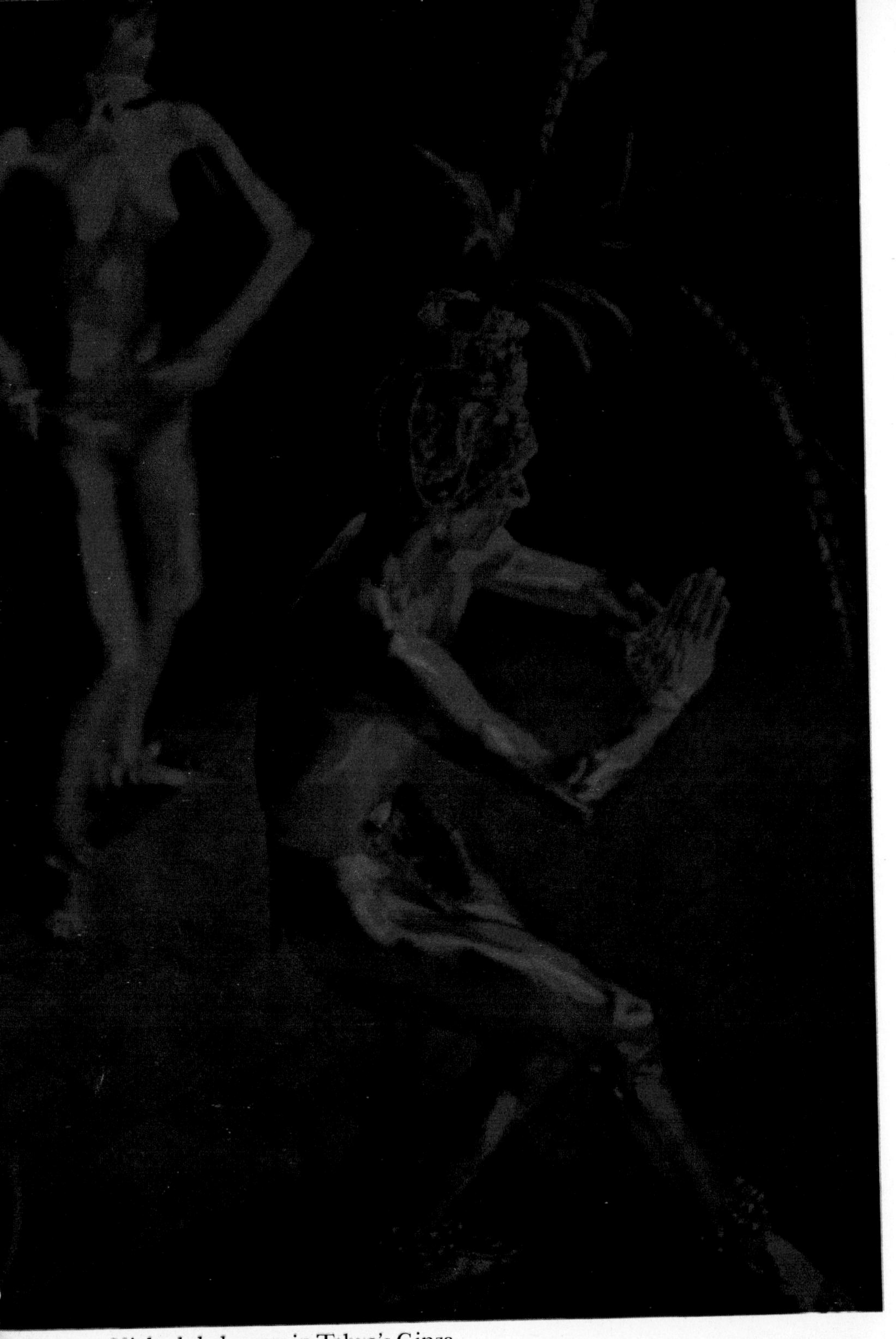

Nightclub dancers in Tokyo's Ginza.

OPPOSITE
Young women in traditional costume.

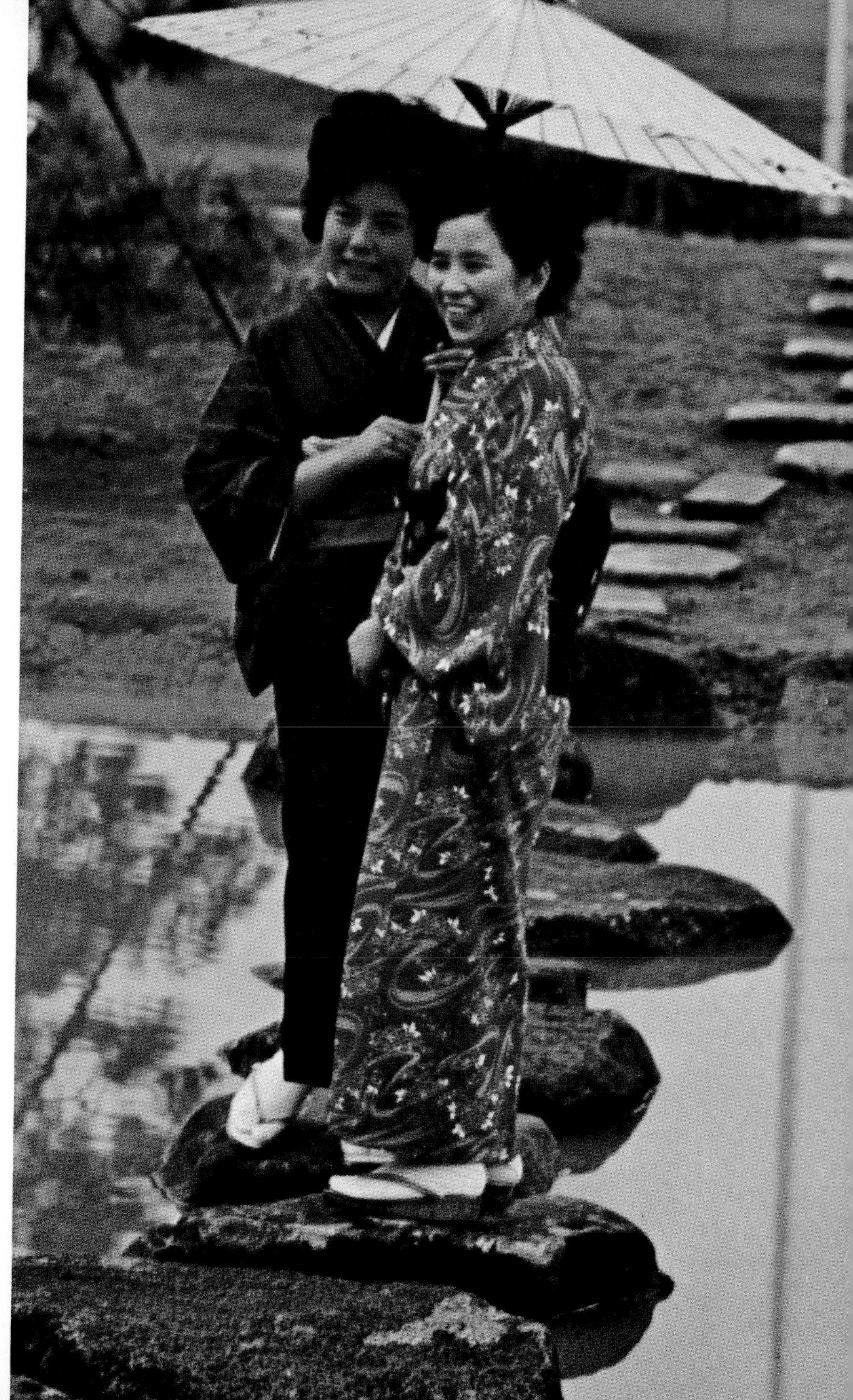

A ninety-one-year-old country woman. Near Nikko.

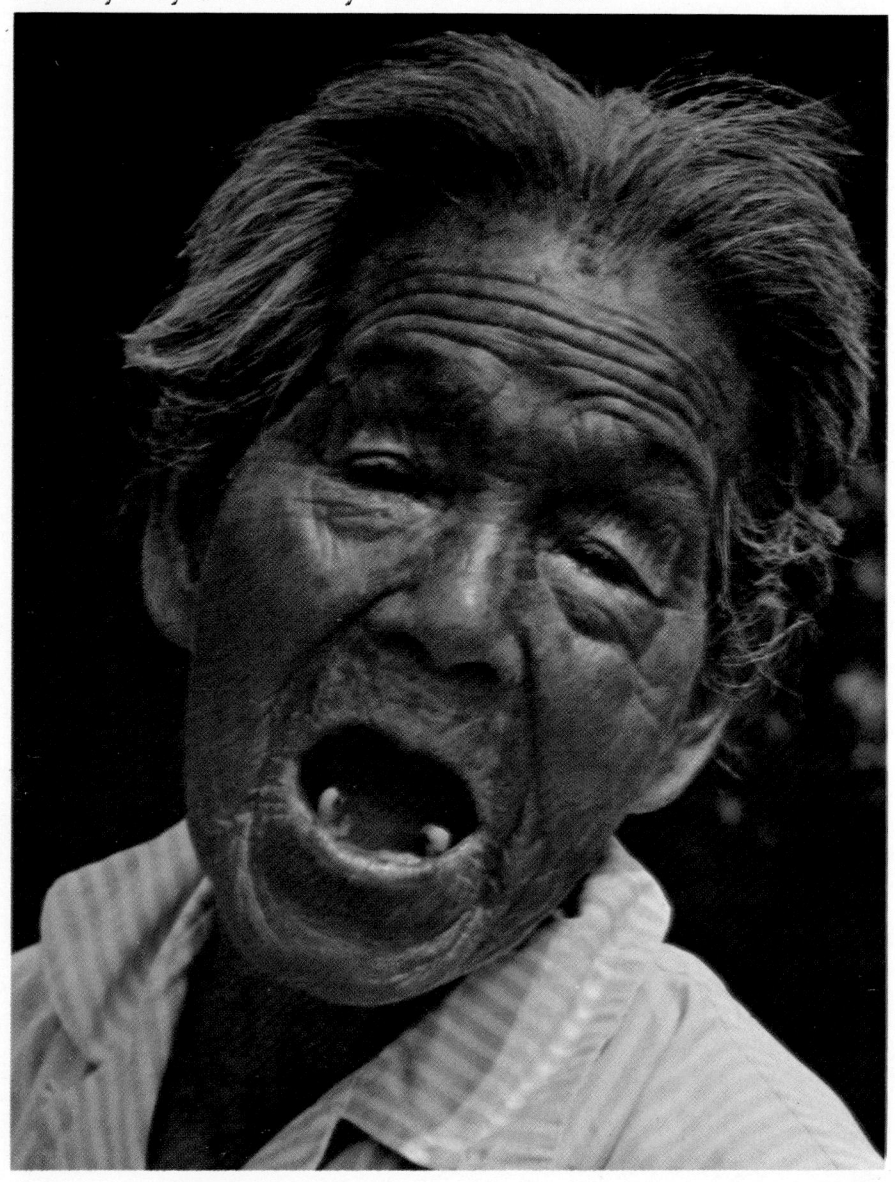

Fashion model. Tokyo.

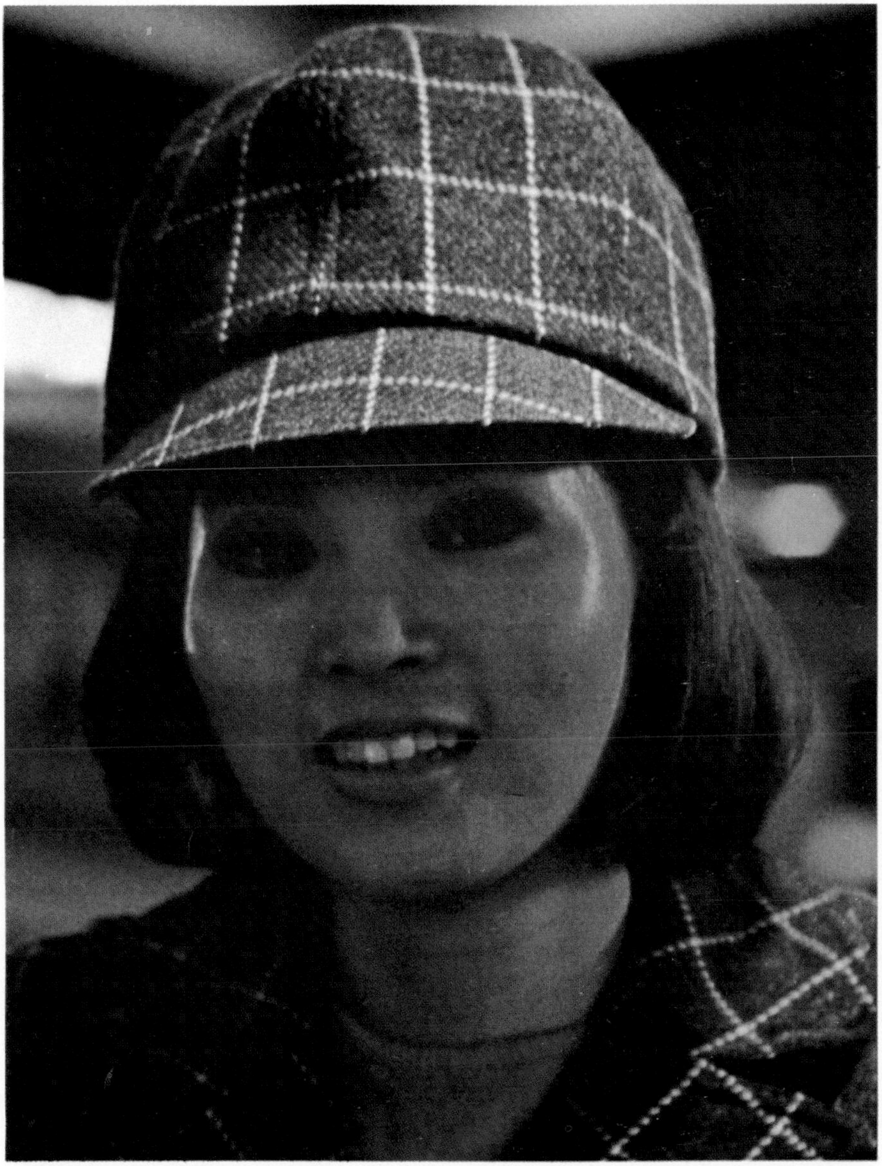

Portrait of a young man.

A bride in ceremonial headdress.

Family portrait taken at a Shinto wedding.

was not a success. In fact, it turned out very badly indeed, and he has now reverted to a charming Japanese girl, quite modern but much more docile than his former wife. What of his parents? There has been a reconciliation, because he had to admit that he had been wrong. He hated to, but he had to. He says himself that it was a cause of great embarrassment to him that his parents were right. Yet all turned out well, because of his admission, and he chose his new bride from a selection offered by his parents. Now he is contentedly back in the family fold with his approved second wife, and satisfaction reigns all around.

Of course, it is not a new thing for youth to try to break away. Japanese poetry is full of hopeless love. Young people in Japan have always been falling in love against their parents' wishes and making the tragic climb up some volcano to take what seemed to be the easiest way out. Now they no longer jump into craters or off bridges as much as they used to. For one thing, suicide is neither so romantic nor so satisfactory a solution as it once seemed, and for another, young people do have more choice than they had before. Perhaps, too, they are coming more and more to realize that what their parents say is true: that marriage is not the end of love, but the beginning.

Yes, the change in Japanese women especially has been unmistakable since the war, so much so that Japanese men make jokes about being henpecked—"Stockings and women are stronger since the war," they say. Yet women still, and I believe voluntarily, yield to the supremacy of the male. Perhaps it is too soon for the custom of the centuries and inherent tradition to be changed by Western example or even by constitutional decrees or labor law revisions. Perhaps women actually enjoy the supremacy of men. Time will tell. At present, however, tradition still holds, especially in the more rural areas such as are to be found in Kyushu, as I myself observed while I lived there.

In Kyushu once I knew a fisherman and his wife, and I met them again not so long ago. I saw change, a little. She was very much the traditional wife, the wife of one of the hard-working fishermen who went out all day and came back tired after their catch. He sat himself down and expected to have his tea served, and his food not just ready on the table but presented to him, and the chopsticks almost put into his hands. My friend still wrung out a hot cloth and wiped his face for him, and wiped his back and his hands, and generally comforted him. In everything she did she took very much the old traditional attitude. She had been working in the fields all day and doing the cooking and the housework, and yet she waited on him as though she had done nothing else all day but look for his return. There was not a great deal of change here, I thought. Yet I did think that she was a little more ready in her talk than she had been before. Certainly she did not maintain silence, as before. Yet when her husband yelled at her to shut up, she still *did* shut up. Some day, though, I thought to myself, she'll say Be quiet yourself, or something like that. She hasn't reached that stage yet, but she's learning. Again, time will tell.

Such tradition still holds in all areas of Japanese life. Change sometimes appears starkly on the surface, and sometimes ripples subtly beneath. Here again is that paradox of Japanese life: change that is not really change. The Japanese woman, for all her progress toward the modern, is still the Japanese woman, a being submissive to the male. She is a more educated woman, a more respected woman. But though the number of women doing post-high-school study has tripled in the last decade and a half, the ratio is still five to one in favor of men. In the all-important prestige schools, such as the universities in Tokyo and Kyoto, the student body is almost exclusively male. The fact is that unless a woman wants to be a teacher or a nurse, college is of little use in helping her to find a job. Her position is comparable to that of American women half a century ago. She is "emancipated" legally but not practically. For instance, while the female working force has doubled since 1953, discriminatory wage scales give them an average monthly salary of 16,000 yen compared to 38,000 yen for the men. The majority of farmhands are unpaid female family workers, just as in prewar times.

In these days of peace and security, Japanese men are tending again to shut out women. There is, I believe, an actual regression from the first flush of emancipation and equality of opportunity following the war, when Japanese men, defeated and discredited, gave way somewhat before their women. True, a few women have gone far in politics—seventeen are members of the House of Councilors. Two others are highly respected atomic scientists. But where the millions are concerned, women remain housewives and mothers.

It is expecting too much, perhaps, to think that after centuries of subjugation, there can be complete change overnight. The change in Japanese women is none the less real, however. It is in the mind and the spirit. She knows now that she is a human being, not more than the man, but certainly not less. She will not force progress, for she does not believe in force, but she will progress. Once the mind is opened to new ideas and new estimates, progress is inevitable.

I pause here to consider an inconsistency. Women in Japan have long had a physical freedom in regard to men that is impossible to Western women. I refer to mixed bathing, not as a sport but as a rite of cleanliness. The Japanese are personally clean. They bathe daily, and while water is not a scarcity, fuel is. It became necessary, centuries ago, to conserve fuel. To heat bath water, fuel is of course essential. Instead of individual baths, communal baths became a national custom, whence it became a habit, first in the family and later in the community. Westerners have been amazed, shocked and diverted, in that order, on seeing men and women bathing together. Mixed bathing continues today, although on a reduced scale. It is usual in spas, and it is still the rule in Hokkaido, as for example in small towns like Noboribetsu.

This is not to say that Japanese men or women are lacking in modesty or self-consciousness. It is rather that they see no cause for shame or embarrassment in the nakedness of the human body, and that for them the causes of modesty and self-consciousness lie elsewhere. What is immodest is to look at a naked man or woman, to stare at certain parts of the anatomy or simply take note of the nakedness. I have seen a man get furious with another man who looked at his wife in the communal bath. The scene that developed was equivalent to a duel. The husband was so outraged by the other man's immodest and insulting act, which in fact was little more than a glance at the woman, that the entire bathhouse was soon in an uproar and the people in charge made them all get out and leave. Ordinarily, nobody looks. One keeps the eyes down and concentrates on bathing oneself.

Once in a while when traveling through villages and countryside on my early visits to Japan I would come upon a stream or brook and find someone enjoying open air and sunshine and bathing naked in the rippling stream. I remember once my children and I chanced upon a lovely young girl taking a bath in a brook. She stood up without a stitch on, utterly unconscious of her body, as much interested in us as we were in her. We had lost our way and we asked her for directions. Quite unembarrassed, she gave them to us. It was of course impossible for us to avoid seeing that she was naked and at the same time quite unnecessary to turn away. In fact, it would have been wrong and tactless; only our awareness would have embarrassed her. It is not, as I say, the nakedness that is immodest; it is the looking.

At another time I was watching fishermen bringing in a heavy haul. It was during the phenomenon that occurs once a year off the coast of Kyushu, when a certain type of small fish comes in toward the coast in great shoals which attract the sharks. The fishermen of Kyushu take out their boats and spread a huge net under the shoals of fish, gathering in both the little fish and the sharks. Then the fishermen haul them in and sort them out, killing the sharks and of course collecting the fish. On this occasion it was warm and the work was arduous. When the boats dragged the net back to the shore they must have been pulling a hundred or even two hundred sharks. The men who pulled that net had to exercise great strength, and they stripped themselves to the skin so that their bodies might be free and unencumbered. No one was conscious at all that they were naked. To all of us watching it seemed the most natural thing in the world for the men to do.

I do remember one occasion when modesty was shown, and to Westerners it must seem like a reverse sort of modesty. A film was being made with a group of female pearl divers, firm-bodied women accustomed to diving with their bodies bare from the waist up. It did not embarrass them, half-naked as they were, to be surrounded by camera crew and extras, nor to be captured by the motion picture camera while in that state. However, it occurred to the American director that the film censors in the States might object to such "nude" scenes, and he asked the women to wear brassières. The divers tried to be cooperative. They put on the brassières. And all at once they became so embarrassed and self-conscious that they could scarcely bring themselves to dive. They were not used to such encumbrances; they were not used to having such attention paid to their breasts, nor thinking of their nakedness.

Indeed, neither Asian men nor women are breast-conscious as are our women and especially our men. Feet are more important to the Asian male than breasts, and in Japan the nape of the neck is considered the most beautiful part of a woman's body.

IN MARRIAGE the relationship between man, woman and children remains traditional, for marriage, as I have said, is still a family business. If the modern Japanese man divides his life between the two worlds of home and business, so may also the Japanese working woman. The neat, efficient secretary in Western dress in an office is as modern, apparently, as if she lived in New York. So, too, is her boss. Yet each, at the end of the day, returns to tradition. That is, she goes home to tidy the house, prepare food and attend to her honored mother-in-law, and he goes to a bar. A bar in itself has little to do with tradition, being an American innovation, but the idea of a place in which men can relax is as old as the oldest geisha house. The bar habit—to me, the great weakness in Japanese society—is a modern evolution and combination of the old, elegant geisha house and the old, inelegant brothel.

When asked why he goes to a bar, the Japanese male will reply that he does business there with other businessmen in a relaxed atmosphere. The atmosphere is certainly relaxed, as I have observed for myself on more than one occasion in Tokyo. Once in particular I was invited by the head of a Japanese firm to accompany him and a few other distinguished gentlemen to his favorite bar at the end of the day. For me the experience was unusual. Our host had telephoned the bar that I was coming, and as I descended from the taxi I was welcomed by the madam, who embraced me warmly, told me she had read my books over and over again and considered me her elder sister. Behind her stood a bevy of pretty girls in kimono, not quite the kind of girls with whom I usually associate. One of them carried a bouquet of flowers, hastily assembled I could see, which she presented to me. All bowed again and again. I made the proper return, they escorted me into the bar and gave me a comfortable chair in an advantageous corner, brought me food and drink, and thereafter surrounded me in a circle, sitting on the floor and oblivious to male guests. I am sure I spoiled the evening for quite a number of men.

Now and then one of the girls would be called away but she always returned when her duties were over, whatever they may have been. We exchanged questions and answers. I learned that most of them were married and had children, that their husbands were day laborers with small incomes, making it necessary for their wives to work. Since this was so, the night work at the bar was a convenience, for the husband could be at home with the children. All agreed that bar work was tedious, for men were the same, wanting to be petted and praised. But it was part of the job, they said, and I could see when they were with the men that they accepted the tousling and fumbling as part of their work and tried to seem pleased. These were, I suppose, rather low class women, but they liked to read—Japan has the highest literacy rate in the world—and they had many questions to ask me about American women, whom they envied because, they said, "American husbands are very sweetly." All of these women spoke simple English.

Observing at last that the men guests were approaching a crisis of rebellion, I urged the young women to go back to work. Thereafter I sat sipping tea instead of sake or Scotch and watched the patient sweetness with which the women poured drinks for and fed food to the men, responding only with pretty smiles when a boisterous man lingered to embrace or reached to pinch their buttocks.

Whatever ideas of sex pervaded the minds of the men, certainly there was no sex in those cool pretty women. If hands became too familiar as liquor flowed, the women quietly withdrew or put the hands aside as a mother might mildly restrain a child. I thought it all rather sad. The madam of this particular place did not permit her girls to have assignations with the men at the bar, and as I say they showed no interest in sex, and the bar on the whole is only a place to make assignations. These places close up at two o'clock, which still leaves enough of the night to go somewhere else, such as a cheap boardinghouse or a hotel. And they do; one has to face the fact that Japanese men are very promiscuous. It must be remembered, too, that the Japanese do not share the Puritan conception of evil in connection with sex. True, Confucianism regarded a man's sex interest in his wife as somewhat indecent, an attitude which influenced the Japanese male, perhaps, but condoned, more or less, his interest in females other than his wife. With Japanese men it is usually "more."

VI

THERE ARE many genuine pleasures in Japanese life, nonetheless. The people of Japan are still prone to melancholy, they are oversensitive to loneliness, and perhaps as a contrast they find pleasure in many ways that have nothing to do with bars or even with sex. They enjoy hobbies and nearly everyone has a hobby of some sort, music, art, photography, books and gardening being the most usual. Rich and poor alike enjoy such pursuits. The meanest house has its bit of garden outside, a few shrubs clipped to a design, a steppingstone or two and perhaps a small bed of raked sand and a tiny pool under a leaning pine. The year with its seasons brings special joys, too. There is a ritual for each season. One should put on long underwear the first of October, for example, and change to a straw hat on the first of July. Change in itself brings pleasure. In a house the alcove called tokonoma reflects the seasons in the flower arrangement and the chosen scroll. Even the Japanese poems called haiku, short though they are, always refer in some way to one of the seasons of the year, and the Japanese people have a tendency to burst into haiku at the drop of a leaf or the first snowflake. For example, the seventeenth-century poet Basho wrote:

The winter storm
Hid in the bamboos
And died away.

And,

The cicada's cry
Gives no sign
That it is about to die.

Basho's disciple, Kikaku, introduced into the haiku a new wit, and succeeded in bringing out the discords of life, and the contrasts and similarities between man and nature:

He is a winter fly,
Disliked,
But long-lived.

Food, too, should be eaten according to season. The refined taste of the Japanese palate rejects foods frozen to be used at any time. For them this is monotony, and monotony they cannot endure. Their love of change shows itself, too, in the changeability of their houses, where walls are movable and rooms serve any purpose. No decoration is immovable and even the tokonoma alcove changes in flowers, arrangements, paintings. Change, yes, but the center is always unchangeable—this, perhaps, is the key to the Japanese character. Thus frugality is a national trait, not only from necessity but for artistic reasons. Japanese art is always spare, fined down to the essential line, yet, this being the principle, Japanese can at the same time be wildly extravagant. Love of beauty, and this love is the secret passion of the Japanese, leads often to extravagance. The principle is observed in a gentleman's wearing a sober black basic, or topcoat, but its lining may be stiff with gold. A woman's kimono may be gray and drab, but its material of the finest and lined with silver. Life appears all simplicity in Japan, but one can spend a thousand dollars more quickly there than anywhere else in the world, I do believe.

Another incongruity is the Japanese attitude toward certain age groups. The middle years, considered the prime of life by Westerners, are almost a desert for the Japanese to cross. Too old to be indulged, too young to command respect, the middle-aged of Japan have many more responsibilities than pleasures. But youth and old age are times of great delight. Except for a China now gone, I am sure Japan is the happiest spot on earth for the old. Little children are loved and indulged, and so are old people. Nor is it a mere sentimental love. Old people are respected for their wisdom and their experience. In any Japanese village one finds enchanting ancients, gay and independent, healthy and free in speech and behavior. They take part in everything with zest and energy, they walk prodigiously, they visit sacred spots on high mountains. They go to Communist meetings and other questionable and controversial places. Indeed, there are usually more old people at such meetings than young ones, for the old know they have nothing to fear. The old are proud of themselves because everyone is proud of them. If they reach ninety or so, they become the darlings of the community. It is a lovely way to end a life.

I came to this conclusion the summer I spent in the village of Kitsu, where we were making a film of my book, *The Big Wave*. Of that adventure I have written elsewhere, but I have not written of the enchanting old men, whom even we could not resist, so that we kept putting them in the picture. Every one of them was escorted to the scene by at least one or two beaming sons, daughters or grandchildren, and usually by a sizable group, all of whom were careful to see that their particular charge had a chair to sit in between scenes, that he looked just right for the cameras, that the sun wasn't too much for him, and that he had his tea at the proper times. And the pride with which each family looked at its own special old man when he was busy acting was heart-warming to see. The old men, of course, took it for granted that they were the stars, and behaved like stars. Shall I ever forget the morning when, in simulated rain, they lined themselves up on the side of a narrow cobbled street and posed for individual pictures? Such self-confidence, such aplomb, can only be the result of assurance of love. And, perhaps, of position, for as long as he lives a man is the head of his house, and a woman never loses her place and influence in the family, whatever her age.

So far as the family is concerned, everything the old folk say is wise. To see these ancients in their homes, surrounded by family, is to see how truly they are adored, how deeply they are respected, how lovingly they are treated. The old one is always offered the first bowl of rice and the choicest tidbits. No draft from open garden door must blow upon him; no discomfort must ever be permitted to ruffle the smooth surface of his life. Every member of the family from baby to father loves him and reveres him, to their mutual benefit. The old ones seem to ripen and blossom because they are happy, and they even seem to possess the wisdom attributed to them. For it is true, of course, that they have had experience with life and they do have many good things to say, and what is more, the family not only listens respectfully but actually solicits their advice. Under such favorable circumstances, wisdom is almost bound to grow. Yes, old age in Japan is something to be looked forward to with eagerness and enjoyed wholeheartedly. It is a shock to realize how untrue this is, for the most part, in our own country, where we are far more inclined to regard the aged as a nuisance.

Family is an endemic concept in Japan and has been so for centuries. This has its roots perhaps in Confucianism, brought over during the centuries from China, and maintained as a means of stability and order in society. The idea of family runs through every organization, from the emperor, who is a sort of father to the nation, to a gang of thieves who will collect themselves around a "father" as head. Although the impact of Americans was severe, yet the idea of the family structure persists.

Even trades are organized in the family pattern. The theatrical profession, the flower arrangers, the musicians, and so on, all have their father heads, persons who stand in a family relation to the others. When a man has mastered an art, for example, he is considered the "son" of the master and is given his master's surname to use. The master's own son inherits the father position, if he is worthy of it. If not, a talented youth is adopted and inherits by reason of his talent. This family organization takes the place of a trade guild. As in a true family, if a member loses his job he is protected by the others and helped until he finds a job again. It is a sort of social security and does indeed do much for the general security of Japanese life. The price is a limiting of the individual. Originality is not encouraged. A young friend of mine, a dancer, lost his position in his "dance family" because he made innovations of his own in his art.

Thus the symbol of Japan, although to a decreasing degree perhaps, is nevertheless the clan in a broad sense, and not just the family clan but a complicated system of many clans, including the clan of the nation itself. The average Japanese finds himself in a world of bewildering allegiances, all requiring some tempering of individuality. Group allegiance is certainly not what it was in feudal days or in prewar Japan. A man gave his life then for lord or emperor. No one today is going to commit hara-kiri for Mitsubishi or Sony Electric. Yet large companies have to some extent replaced the feudal lords. There is the same loyalty on the one hand, the same perpetual care on the other, and the same submerging of the individual.

The true family unit, the domestic family, has changed less than any other. A child is expected to be grateful to his parents for having been given life, and to show his gratitude by respectful behavior. His duty to the family is to make of himself a successful person, so that his family may gain prestige. I am sure that there are times when this family obligation is irksome upon the young and limiting to personal freedom. On the other hand, it means that the individual is never lonely. No one is lonely in Japan, young or old, insofar as the company of other persons goes, at least, for one is surrounded from birth to death. True, modern young men, living in Tokyo, for example, seem to break away as young men do, but there seems always to be a return. I think first of my radio commentator friend, who broke away and then returned, and then of young Wasaburo, whose ambition to be independent carried him to the United States. His parents wrote me of his coming and begged me to keep an eye on him in New York. It was impossible, for Wasaburo wanted no eye on him and I gave up after a few months. Yet it was only a year later that his parents wrote to tell me that their son had returned to the family, had been exemplary through a family crisis, all of which they attributed to the beneficent influence of the United States. What happened, of course, was that Wasaburo discovered that without family, life was dull and dangerous in its loneliness.

In this respect the youth of Japan are quite unlike the youth of America. In the United States many young people want to be in business for themselves, whereas young Japanese prefer to join one of the huge prestige companies, *zaibatsu,* where they will be secure for the rest of their lives, still samurai dependent on their overlords. American young people seem anxious to leave home and become independent, while Japanese often prefer to remain with the family, even after marriage. There are emotional and practical reasons for this. On the one hand, the ancient ties of obligation and respect still hold the members of a family very close. On the other, credit is hard come by in Japan, and, therefore, many young people cannot break away even if they wish to do so.

Another undeniable fact is that Japanese firms prefer to employ graduates from certain favored universities, however qualified other applicants appear to be. Many companies in Japan are known as Tokyo University firms, or Waseda or Keio firms, and so on, meaning of course that graduates of a particular school have priority in a particular company. It is all rather like the old-school-tie system in England. The top six universities in Japan, five of which are in Tokyo, are Tokyo University, Kyoto University, Keio, Waseda, Tokyo Kodai and Hitotsubashi. In the spring of 1964 the 300 biggest companies in Japan took an amazing 94.8 per cent of their 14,000 new employees from these six universities. When one realizes that there are 245 universities in Japan, one understands the enormity of the problem for students from the less favored universities. And of course it must be understood that when one is talking about Japanese students, one is talking largely about the male. Women, as I have said, constitute a small minority in Japanese universities and are still heavily discriminated against by Japanese employers.

One result of attending a university whose graduates are

favored by big business is a certain overconfidence and casualness on the part of the students. The most favored university of all is, of course, Tokyo. There is a Todai (Tokyo University) song which translated is something like this:

> When a Todai man is standing, he is playing pachinko. When he is sitting, he is enjoying mahjong. And when he is walking, he is heading for the bicycle race track.

Not all students at Japan's top universities are pleasure hunters, but it cannot be denied that many of them are. And perhaps the freshman, at least, can be excused. After all, he has just passed an entrance examination that began, for all practical purposes, when he was born. For Todai students the future is assured. They have eight years to complete a four-year course, under what amounts virtually to a no-flunk policy, and after graduation the Big Business jobs will be waiting. Or so they hope, for this is beginning to change. Of late, jobs in Japan have become scarce even for the most favored graduates. Perhaps the Todai student, too, will soon find himself spending less time on pachinko, mahjong, and the race track.

The presence of many of these college boys in protest marches around Tokyo as members of the Zengakuren demo must be explained in part, at least, by their having too much time on their hands, for few, really, have less to protest than they. On the other hand, it must be said in all fairness that Japanese students of today are acutely aware of the world's problems and that their vociferous demonstrations are nearly always intelligent protests in the cause of peace. And in this respect, at least, they are much like college students nearly everywhere in the world.

No, rebellious youth in Japan is not different from rebellious youth the world over. Much that one reads in the papers and sees in the movies about the "lost" youth of Japan is exaggerated. Some may behave blindly sometimes, like those who on occasion attempt to burn down the Diet and tangle with the police. Some may be materialistic, restless, with little confidence in the future. But in such contacts as I have had with Japanese college youth I have found them to be, in general, a very serious lot; introspective, somewhat pessimistic, the majority dedicated to learning, pluggers but not creators, agnostic, but hardly "lost" except in the narrowest Christian sense. Of course they question traditional values, but where in the world is it otherwise?

One thing is certain. No matter how iconoclastic they may be during their college days, they will become conservative the moment they put on the tailored gray mufti of zaibatsu, as most of them will. Like Wasaburo, they will return to the bosom of the family, to become authoritative fathers and responsible members of the community.

In the hierarchy that is the Japanese family system, each person has position and therefore an honorific title. One does not speak to brother number three as one does to brother number two or one. This is difficult for a foreigner, but instinctive to a Japanese, who knows exactly the level of approach for each human being. It is a situation characteristic of old and stratified cultures and has its own advantages. A certain ease follows when one knows where one stands in relation to other persons. One is not dependent upon the vagaries of love and friendship since the family surrounds. Whether this can continue as Japan becomes industrialized and altogether modern cannot be foretold. It is an axiom, apparently a Western axiom, that freedom for the individual brings with it the penalty of loneliness.

It is true, too, that under the Japanese system severe demands are made of each member of a family. I think of my friend who is the wife and active business partner of a great motion picture magnate in Tokyo. I weekend at their house outside the city, and I know her both in her office and at home. She wears kimono at all times, a contrast to most Japanese businesswomen, and looks exotic in a quiet way, certainly thoroughly Oriental, although her office is as modern as any in a glass house in New York, and her half-dozen secretaries are as smart as their American counterparts. She conducts an international motion picture company and thinks nothing of taking a jet for a few days in Paris, Rome or London. Yet her family life is centered about her husband's old mother, the last of that generation, and her daughter is a talented young actress. In short, while her daily life is modern and extremely successful, her roots are solidly in Japanese traditional life.

Her house is typical of a dichotomy that has no division, its meeting point a smooth passing from one part to the other. Thus we enter through a gate in a wall, and the gate is barred. A bell brings the gateman to open it, and we are in a garden, a Japanese garden complete with rocks, a pool and stone lanterns well placed. The house is large, in the main Japanese, but with a modern garage for the family Rolls-Royce, the daughter's sports car and the workaday station wagon. The house when we enter it seems entirely Western except that we take off our shoes at the door and accept slippers from a maid in kimono who kneels to put them on our feet. We are ushered, with many bows from the little maid, into the living room. It is furnished entirely in the Western style, and very handsomely, as are the dining room beyond and the library across the hall.

But wait—all these rooms open into a central room which looks as though it came out of a museum of old Japan. The floor is covered by tatami mats instead of carpets. In the middle sits a little old lady on her floor cushion before a table barely above the floor. She is eating her supper, a Japanese meal served by an elderly Japanese maid in kimono, who kneels as she opens the canister of hot rice. She fills a bowl and sets it on the table where three or four dishes are waiting, a small whole fish baked on a flat stone, some green vegetables, and sliced octopus.

"My honored mother-in-law," my friend says.

I bow, the old lady smiles and nods affably, but does not rise. My friend explains.

"Our mother prefers the Japanese style of living, but we like her with us and she enjoys everything. So she is here in the heart of our home."

This is of course a wealthy home. Yet the same atmosphere, generally speaking, pervades even a poor home. Each generation respects and considers the other; each in its time trusts the other, and feels secure. Thus it is with my friends the Kosakais, who have never so much as seen a Rolls-Royce or a dining room suite.

The Kosakai family lives in central Honshu, in the town of Inuyama through which the Kiso River flows. They have lived in Inuyama for over three hundred years, and so have many other Kosakais. There are ninety-eight families in forty-six houses bearing the Kosakai name. Such family concentration is not unusual; rather, it is typical of this rural part of Japan. Not long ago I went back to see the Kosakais in their hundred-year-old house. Cypress wood inside and outside was black with age and had never known paint or any preservatives. Portions of the exterior were of thick mud-plaster and the roof was part slate tile and part matted cypress bark, two feet thick. Though I was not expected, the mother managed a lunch of eggs, rice, soup, fish and spinach, which we ate in a tatami room opening out toward the Kosakai rice fields and the distant mountains.

The rest of the house was dark and primitive, particularly the kitchen and *obenjo*. An ancient wood-burning stove was in the former, and in the latter a box for catching the excrement, later to be used for fertilizer. Despite a vastly increased use of chemicals, small farmers in Japan and other Far Eastern countries still fertilize their fields with "night soil." It is a time-tested and time-honored method of enriching the soil, and one that is being encouraged in this modern world by Japanese scientists who are working to find satisfactory ways to disinfect and make better use of this humble material. The head of this Kosakai family, unaware of the advances of science and uninterested in modern conveniences, obviously prefers the old ways. His life, like his house, is that of his ancestors. Yet there is great warmth both in his house and his life, a great togetherness of brothers, sisters, sons, daughters, uncles, aunts, cousins, nephews, with never a thought that old or young might possibly be "in the way." Daughter-in-law lives with them in the house, and harmony reigns.

It is quite true that discords can and do arise when a girl marries into a home and is obliged to defer to her mother-in-law, which of course she must do. I think of a friend in Japan, a talented writer now in her mid-life, who had an extremely difficult time with her husband's mother. My friend, at the time of her marriage, was one of the more emancipated people, a very modern woman educated in the United States and a graduate of one of our American colleges. She stayed unmarried for a rather unusually long time, and when she finally fell in love—yes, she fell in love, and decided to marry for love—it was with a widower who lived with his children and his mother. When my friend had made her choice she went to friends who arranged matters for her. I might mention here that this is another freedom that the Japanese woman has: If she has an inclination for a particular man, she does not need to wait for his overtures but is free to ask her parents or a go-between to approach the man on her behalf. It is all considered perfectly proper, and a very sensible way of finding out whether or not feelings are reciprocated. In this case my friend's feelings were reciprocated and the marriage was arranged. There was a fine relationship between the two of them, and she made a very good Japanese wife even though she had been educated abroad.

But her husband's home proved to be too traditional for her. The old mother-in-law dominated both her and the children, and treated my friend as though she had had no experience or education at all. This of course irked her. There was polite battle after polite battle, and the younger woman was always on the losing end. The old mother would insist, for instance, that the children be given certain kinds of food that their own mother knew they should not have, and would permit them to do certain things that the mother would have preferred them not to do. There was no arguing with the old lady, other than the barest of remonstrances, for after all she was honored mother-in-law and she was to be respected. Her wishes were law. To make things even more difficult, the man always took his mother's part. It was a son's duty, and he did his duty. His wife recognized that he was correct in doing so, but it made her feel very solitary. She was obliged to yield over and over and over again to the autocratic old woman, until her position became almost insupportable. As a matter of fact she wrote a book, published in this country, and part of it related the troubles she had had with the old woman and the deep resentment that had grown within her.

On the other hand, I know a woman who was able to arrange things much more satisfactorily. She is truly Japanese, never having been outside her own country, and she happens to have quite a strong personality. The mother-in-law, in her turn, is rather submissive. There have been clashes of will, but the younger woman nearly always triumphs. She is fortunate, too, in having a husband who loves her more than he loves his mother, so that he tries very hard to be fair, or perhaps more than fair, to his wife in spite of the traditional respect for elders. I must say that here we

Americans have had an effect upon Japanese custom. These days, in spite of tradition, there is an expectation of companionship and love to be found in marriage, and the husbands of today are somewhat more inclined to take the part of their wives.

Of course, one of the great delights in life for a daughter-in-law is to become a mother-in-law in her turn. Then a woman truly comes into her own. What she is like as a mother-in-law depends very much on what her own mother-in-law was like. If her mother-in-law was sweet and gentle, then she herself is likely to be sweet and gentle when time and circumstance promote her to that favored position. But if her husband's mother has been domineering and dictatorial, then—let her own son's wife beware!

On the whole, though, the Japanese family system operates with a minimum of friction. Love and respect are the rule, rather than the exception, and the closeness of family life is a great unifying force in the nation. Whether it can continue in its present form remains to be seen. Yet I feel it can and will, for it is within Japanese history and tradition to keep their ancient central structure while they change all else. Our American way of life has developed from an entirely different ancestry and history. Our ancestors parted from their families, left their countries, usually as rebels, and carved a nation out of a wilderness. They cut their roots. Meantime, before they could establish new and unchanging family ties, to be developed through the centuries, the industrial age overtook them. What has happened in this new environment to a new people need not necessarily happen to an old people whose roots are undisturbed. It is said that no family system can persist in an industrialized society. But it is possible that Japan, the most modern nation in ancient Asia and the most ancient of those nations allied with the modern West, may refute the saying.

VII

WHILE I WRITE so confidently of the solid structure of the family in Japanese society, I think also of Japanese women, old and new, who from their wedding days know that their relationships to their husbands are threatened by other women who have chosen another way of life, one as ancient as marriage itself, the women who are the companions of men, but not their wives. They are the geisha, and are not to be confused with bar girls.

Geisha houses have an elegance all their own, for they are the houses of ladies. A man cannot simply arrive there as he would at a brothel. Proper introductions must be presented. Nor is the geisha house a hotel. The geisha does not sleep there. It is a place of entertainment for men and women.

When I was in Tokyo, my friend, the motion picture star Sessue Hayakawa, gave a handsome geisha party. All the guests were Japanese except for an American couple and myself. The geisha house was immense and beautifully furnished in Japanese style. Maids removed our shoes and put slippers on our feet before we mounted the polished stairs to a huge room. The shoji were drawn and lanterns lit the scene. A great low table occupied the middle of the tatami floor and floor cushions surrounded it. We were the last to arrive, and the geisha fluttered about, helping us to be seated. To each of us, man and woman alike, a geisha was assigned to kneel, not quite beside us, but at the right elbow. Mine was a pretty woman in a brilliant brocaded kimono, her hair down in winged old-fashioned style. She spoke a little English and prattled about my books, some of which she had read in Japanese, and while she talked she poured tea and offered small sweetmeats. I felt shy and a little strange to be so attended, but she was correct in her behavior toward me. It amused me, indeed, to see how differently the geisha behaved to a female guest, almost as to an older sister.

Nor was there undue familiarity with a man. The geisha sits very close to the man she serves, her knee pressing his side, perhaps, and from time to time she may touch his hand playfully, but nothing more. Her face is nicely made up, she has on layers of garments under her bright kimono and heavy obi, and is therefore somewhat inaccessible. I have always been told that geisha are talented and trained conversationalists, but I do not know this for myself, since I speak no Japanese and certainly they are not trained in English—at least not the one assigned to me. I imagine that they suit their conversation to the guest, and it may therefore be quite proper or quite risqué. They are trained to please.

What I do enjoy about geisha is their dancing. The word "geisha" means *artist,* and many of them are artists in the dance. Singing and playing a musical instrument, usually the samisen, are also enjoyable to hear, but I like the dance, the smooth graceful movements, the flying long sleeves of kimono, the fluttering of fans. These dances are never voluptuous as are so many Western dances. On the evening of Sessue Hayakawa's invitation the best dancing was performed by a geisha who must have been at least fifty years old. Hers were stylized dances, taken perhaps from *no* plays, or at least adapted from them. They were beautiful but dignified. Young geisha, or *maiko,* usually dance with some gaiety, but there was none that night. I remember one of the guests was a great sumo wrestling champion, a star in his profession, a huge fellow weighing nearly four hundred pounds. He left early for a practice fight and before he went he shook hands with each of us who were Americans. I had never seen such a hand. It was like an elephant's pad, thick, soft and strong. My hand disappeared into it. I had a moment's panic as I felt that all-enveloping clasp, but when I looked up, far up, it was to see gentle eyes in the vast immobile face. Another of Japan's contrasts!

A geisha apprentice is often the child of a geisha, though sometimes an orphan or a girl who simply prefers this life and is trained for about four years for the Geisha Union examinations. After passing them, she is ready for what might politely be referred to as her "graduation ceremony." A wealthy connoisseur usually performs the rite, though the girl must agree to him and she may even select him herself from among the ever-present applicants.

There is a real difference between a geisha and a prostitute, although occasionally the one may become the other. If the geisha accepts protection from a man, however, it is usually to become his mistress. She may even become his wife. Today the geisha have resumed their old dignity after some debasement during the war. A geisha does not usually earn her living by sexual favors, although she may spend too much money on her clothes, for of course she must be beautifully and expensively dressed, and in order to pay her debts she may have to accept men she would not otherwise accept. There has always been much romance in Japan about the geisha and even about the prostitute. After all, they were the women with whom men could communicate. Marriages were family affairs. A wife could and did produce the necessary and desired children without becoming a confidante or even a friend. Her place was prescribed. In some ways she was almost like a personal servant, though an upper one. Something of this still clings to the relationship. A wife's manners and speech are shaped by tradition; she seldom speaks her mind within the seclusion of her home, although she has become quite outspoken in community affairs, and life with her is perhaps somewhat dull. The freedom of communication with a geisha offers a more exciting possibility, or so I imagine.

Throughout the centuries, before her encounter with the American male, the Japanese woman had known only the Japanese man. She had taken as a matter of course her subjection to him; she had only one choice to make in regard to the relationship: she could choose to be a wife or a geisha. Did she choose to be a wife, she was the mother of his children, the keeper of his house. The house was her domain, in such case, and he was absolute master. She waited while he took his meals, she was silent until he spoke, she sat up until he chose to come home, she tended his every comfort. Did she choose the other relationship, she renounced the security of being his wife, and became instead a geisha at the highest level and a prostitute at the lowest.

Both geisha and prostitute were without security, and each had her place in the man's scheme of things. The prostitute needed only to be sexually adept. But the geisha had to be educated to be an intellectual companion to men of intellect and a companion in art to men of artistic talent. She had to be learned and she had to be accomplished in the arts. Such an education could only be acquired by a gifted woman, and so highly gifted that many a geisha became famous in her own right. Nor did she receive men in her own house. She entertained in houses where men gathered; and by conversation and music, both vocal and instrumental, by delicate attentions, never grossly sensual, she made the time pass pleasantly at least, and often with enchantment, for her skill in suggesting the romantic possibilities between man and woman was, and is, part of her education.

If the relationship deepened with any one man, it was only by her choice, and he maintained her in a separate house. Occasionally he even married her, but it was not expected. The poetic love stories of Japan, in contrast to those of China, center about the romantic attachment between a geisha and her lover. In China an erotic attachment usually, or often, ends by the girl being brought into the man's home as a concubine. In Japan these two areas, family and erotic love, are kept separate. A Japanese man marries the woman his parents have chosen in order to carry on the family through children. His "human feelings," and such feelings are always permissible in Japan, are fulfilled through his relationships with other women in the other area. Moreover, such relationships may hold some security for the other woman. A geisha, if she decides to accept a man, requires him to sign a contract with her, setting forth what he will provide for her, and the length of time he will continue to do so. Sometimes, of course, she falls in love and gives herself without contract, in which case she takes the risk.

All this is accepted matter-of-factly by both men and women, though, of course, with some private reservations on the part of the women. The Japanese attitude toward sex in all its forms is far more permissive than it is in the West. Sex impulses—"human feelings"—are taken as a matter of course and arouse no special excitement or comment. Pornography is not looked upon as a sin or even as vulgarity, and eroticism is naturalism. Children are not prevented from masturbation, nor is it considered important one way or the other. In the adult, autoeroticism is merely a form of private relief and nobody's business. It, too, is unimportant and therefore no guilt is connected with it, although a person of decorous life and individual maturity would not allow it to assume a significant place in his life. Homosexuality, also, is accepted in Japan as "human feeling." Traditionally even men in high places could practice homosexuality, since "human feeling" is outside the realm of censure. This non-moralistic attitude still prevails, although in the Meiji period, when Japan discovered how the West felt about homosexuality, she did pass laws making it illegal and therefore punishable. Such laws contradicted their acceptance of "human feelings" and were not obeyed. In Japanese eyes homosexuality is shocking only when it takes place between adults, for the self-respecting Japanese male considers it beneath his dignity to accept the passive role and act as a woman. For them this role is assumed only by boys. Intoxication is also understandable to the Japanese mind as part of "human feelings." He will not deny himself the pleasurable relaxation of getting drunk occasionally when the occasion is suitable, any more than he would deny himself the pleasure of an evening with a geisha or prostitute. But a sane man will not carry drunkenness or sexuality to so absurd a degree as to disturb his own life or his family life. If he were to allow either pleasure to absorb his time or strength to the extent of disturbing his business or family life, his sanity would be seriously questioned. His morals would not even be discussed. In short, in Japanese life neither drunkenness nor sexuality is directly related to morality. Sex, above all, is presumed to be a natural need, to be satisfied in the way that a person finds most suitable for himself. A good wife, as the member of the family in charge of household accounts, pays her husband's brothel and bar bills and makes no complaint.

Does she not grieve? Once I was with a group of Japanese women and we were talking of our feelings about men and women.

"Do you mind when your husband sleeps with another woman?" I asked.

We discussed their various answers at length. The conclusion we came to was the same that would have been made by a group of Western women. My friend Haruko put it succinctly.

"If a woman loves her husband, she suffers," she said.

Once upon a time in China I put the same question and the answer was the same, in spite of tradition and years of habit and custom. The human heart is the same everywhere in the world.

Yet my friend Haruko, modern woman though she is, and possessed of her own "human feelings," still sees to it that her husband, a prosperous businessman in Osaka, looks neat when he goes for the evening to a geisha house with his associates. He is a handsome man and it is a matter of pride with her that he looks his best for other women, as a credit to his wife.

If he looks at her with a certain smile before he leaves, she understands.

"If I am late, don't wait," he tells her.

"Enjoy yourself," she replies.

Of course she does wait. But the days of her tears are over. When he comes in looking—what shall I say, refreshed?—she is amiable and pours him his bowl of tea without a word of reproach. Life for her is divided into two separate areas, her own and the other woman's, and within her own area she is secure, if not always content.

Whether the Japanese woman is content with her lot depends entirely on how Western she has become. My friend Setsu, who is a Nisei, born in the United States and returned to Japan, is not at all content with her Japanese husband, a physician, handsome and successful. They have quarrelled over his coming home in the small hours of the morning, and he won by not coming home at all. She now waits up for him exactly as Haruko does for her husband.

"Do you mind?" I inquired of Setsu.

"Of course I mind, but what can I do?" she replied with American indignation.

Thus the Japanese split-level existence: the man, on the one hand an honored father and respected businessman, on the other a male whose "human feelings" are to be indulged; the woman, on the one hand a wife and mother with a voice in P.T.A. meetings, neighborhood affairs and the business world, and on the other a female whose duty it is to accept the feminine, submissive role and devote herself to pleasing the male.

It was into this clearly defined relationship, traditional in Japan between man and woman, that the American man came, and looked about him with a delight approaching awe. Whatever he expected to find in Japan it was not the Japanese woman he found. Whatever she expected to find in the American conquerors it was not the one she found. It is fascinating to reflect upon the meeting of these two, and the attachments that developed between them in the glow of their mutual surprise.

What he found was a compliant, gay female who was enchanted by him, and in return gave him her response, and one so ready, so complete, that he felt for the first time he had discovered woman. And she knew him as he had never been known, it seemed. She knew his maleness, she knew how to make him comfortable, how to serve him in small delightful ways, how to coax away a headache with tender hands, how to massage his tired feet, how to take off his stiff Western uniform and slip on a soft cotton *yukata*. There in the quiet of a few small rooms he was lord and master as he had never been in his life. For here was a woman whose delight was in making him content not only with her but with himself. She did not distinguish between a contented body and a contented mind. She knew that the two go together and that happiness is a total state. Whatever he wanted was what she gave. She could be a consoling nurse, a gay companion, a passionate lover. With all her demureness, she had no sexual inhibitions, trained as she had been in Japanese naturalism.

And he—what did he give her? He gave her a courtesy, a consideration, she had never known before. He made her feel precious and lovable, a pet to be teased in gaiety and play, a creature to be adored and marveled over, above all a woman to be protected and treasured and made happy. She had not thought herself valuable. Now she knew she was. It was a mutual discovery, and no wonder there was so much lovemaking. Alas, there were many children born out of wedlock, children belonging wholly neither to Japan nor the United States and yet to both. These are the new people, inevitable when two peoples meet in war and love and the world does not know what to do with them. In Japan, as elsewhere, they constitute a sore problem, as yet unsolved. Meanwhile the love between man and woman works its magic, bringing the people inevitably together. The area of "human feelings," so much a part of Japanese thought and philosophy, influences West as well as East, in spite of the fact that both are reluctant to accept the new child that such "human feelings" produce, the child who is born too soon, a stranger in our world.

But to return, in conclusion, to the geisha, who may very well also be, someday, a stranger in our world. The true geisha is no sexual plaything for the sensation-seeking male, either Japanese or Western. She is the "other woman," so resented by the one who sits at home and waits, but she is the one with the union card, who has studied hard and passed examinations to reach her position. She is also apt to be more talented in the arts than her less mature and less genuine, if sometimes prettier, modern competitor, the bar girl, and she will not entertain outside of legitimate geisha establishments. These today are maintained largely for tourists or Japanese executives over fifty, although, as I say, they still have some appeal for younger men. In twenty years the geisha may be extinct, for the tastes of Japanese men are changing. Like his Western brothers, the Japanese man is beginning to enjoy a more obvious and physical companionship with women. Now that the modern strip tease has reached Japan, as a strictly American innovation, the Japanese, always naturalistic when it comes to the body bare, goes to the extreme. He wants the strip-teaser to disrobe completely, and that also is not enough. He wishes to see her perform her naked tricks, such as gymnastic maneuvers with her pelvic muscles, and he wants to see lewd exhibitionism. There is, I observe, a certain childishness in all this, or at least an adolescent state of mind. The Japanese man has not yet learned to enjoy woman as a human being.

Yet, by contrast, life within the family itself remains singularly pure and traditional. Parents are respected, and children are warmly loved and seldom punished. In all the many times I have visited Japan I have never seen a child beaten or even spanked. No, wait—once when I was walking along a country road I heard a loud pretentious bawling, and turning a corner I came upon a village mother beating her son of about eight or ten years old with a short-handled broom. He

OPPOSITE
Farming near the Pacific Ocean.

Binding wheat. Hokkaido.

A rural character.

In villages and rural towns, life continues to follow the old ways.

Cowherds, near Mount Aso. Kyushu.

Road repair gang. Honshu.

Village woman with her children. Southern Kyushu.

Man from a mountain village.
Near Sendai, northern Honshu.

Fishing along a small river. Northern Honshu.

Men and women work their fruitful land, tilling the soil, watching over their herds...

On a country road. Near Aomori, Honshu.

On a farm in Kita-Hiroshima. Hokkaido.

Harrowing. Southern Kyushu.

Fisherman casting his net.

...men and nature follow the ancient rhythm of the seasons.

Sawing wood. Northern Honshu.

In the towns, a new spirit is more evident.

Apothecary shop. Kyoto.

Entrance to a movie house.

The apothecary now has a modern shop window, the soothsayer sets up on a busy street alongside the movie theater.

A street fortune teller with customer. Hiroshima.

Market women. Nagasaki.

Vegetable woman. Aomori, Honshu.

People stream to work, to the markets and their daily pursuits.

Office workers en route to work. Tokyo.

Street scene. Tokyo.

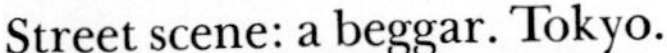

Selling fireworks. Northern Honshu.

Street scene: a beggar. Tokyo.

Fish market: octopus stall. Tokyo.

Night scene: the entertainment district. Tokyo.

Day and night the streets teem with life.

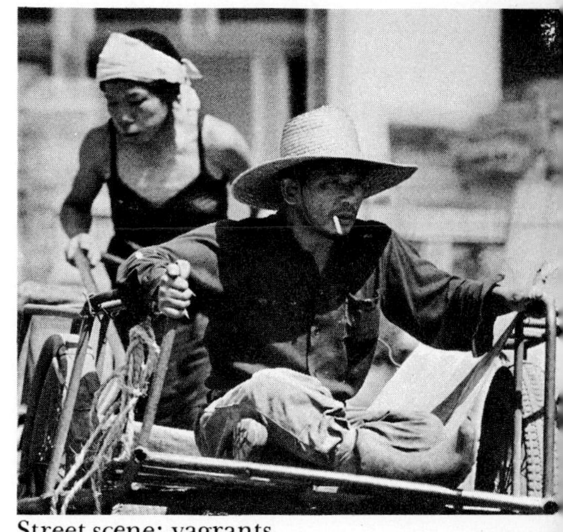

Street scene: vagrants.
Near Aomori, Honshu.

LEFT
Night scene. Hokkaido.
Window shopping. Kyushu.

BELOW
Street scene. Tokyo.
Young hikers. Tokyo.

had evidently loitered on his way home from school, for his knapsack was on his shoulder.

The moment she saw me she stopped to stare, and so did the boy. Something about me amused them for they burst into simultaneous laughter and went together into their house. The broom lay in the dust. I picked it up and it was made of soft rice straw and could not have hurt a kitten.

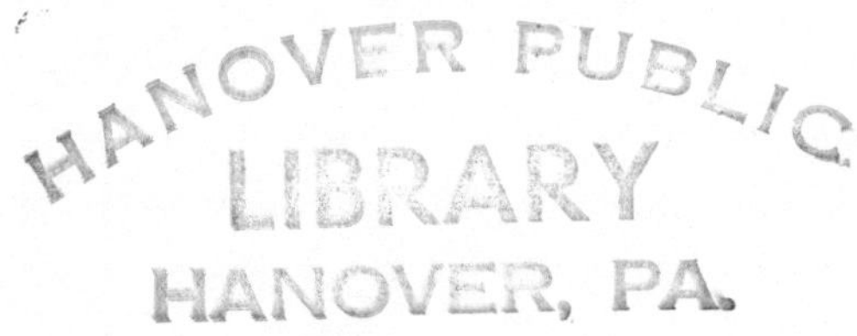

VIII

It is interesting to reflect for a moment upon the differences in the areas of moral feeling and standards in the peoples of Japan and the United States. Americans divide these areas somewhat rigidly into spirit and flesh, the two being in opposition in the life of a human being. Ideally spirit should prevail but all too often it is the flesh that does prevail. The Japanese make no such division, at least between one as good and the other as evil. They believe that a person has two souls, each necessary. One is the "gentle" soul, the other is the "rough" soul. Sometimes the person uses his gentle soul, sometimes he must use his rough soul. He does not favor his gentle soul, neither does he fight his rough soul. Human nature in itself is good, Japanese philosophers insist, and a human being does not need to fight any part of himself. He has only to learn how to use each soul properly at the appropriate times. Virtue for the Japanese consists in fulfilling one's obligations to others. Happy endings, either in life or in fiction, are neither necessary nor expected, since the fulfillment of duty provides the satisfying end, whatever the tragedy it inflicts. And duty includes a person's obligations to those who have conferred benefits upon him and to himself as an individual of honor. He develops through this double sense of duty a self-discipline which is at once permissive and rigid, depending upon the area in which it is functioning.

The process of acquiring this self-discipline begins in childhood. Indeed, one may say it begins at birth. Let me illustrate by telling the story of my friends, the Matsumoto family. That is not their name in fact, for it would not be fair of me to reveal the details of my delightful stay in their home on the distant outskirts of Tokyo. There in a pleasant country house I spent long quiet months, my window open to distant hills. The family was one of three generations, the eldest rooted in ancient traditions; the second headed by the oldest son, a young scientist already famous in his study of the ionosphere; the third two gay children, boy and girl, who went off every morning in immaculate Western garb. A third child was expected and in fact was born within the first week of my arrival, a second son, very plump and healthy. My friend Sumiko refused to go to the hospital because she wanted the baby born under the ancestral roof, as the others had been, and thus he was born at home on a fine spring morning. I was interested in the welcome he received. Of course every happy family, East or West, welcomes a new baby, but in Japan the couple are thinking, too, of their duty to carry on the family. Without children they feel they have failed as human beings and as a married pair. Hideki, the baby's father, was especially gratified to have a second son.

"True, I have one son," he said, "but two are safer. One

never knows. And now I can be reasonably sure that there will be a son to tend my tomb, and preserve our family honor. I have done my duty as a father in producing him and he will do his duty in being my son."

Three children made the mother secure, too. Japanese women do not want to be childless. They feel a spiritual obligation to produce children. The obligation is still strong, in spite of the fact that Japan has now stabilized her population, although in the thirties her birth rate was almost twice that of the United States. I was interested in Sumiko's preparation for her new baby. The birth itself was very private and Sumiko did not utter a cry while she was in labor, lest people know what was going on. Indeed my room was only across a small garden from hers, but I heard not a sound until Hideki himself explained that Sumiko would not be present at the evening meal because she had given birth.

When I was invited the next day to inspect the new baby he was lying on a little pallet bed near Sumiko. I had seen the baby's bed earlier, for Sumiko herself had prepared the new covers and quilt, making them of silk and down as soft as the breast of a singing bird. A baby is more comfortable in its own bed, Sumiko had explained, although it should be near the mother.

"He should feel independent from birth," Hideki had announced.

"He will creep into my bed one of these days of his own free will when he is old enough to know that I am his mother," Sumiko had replied.

So early is the Japanese child given his own identity! If I were to define in a word the attitude of the Japanese toward their children I would put it in one succinct word—"respect." Love? Yes, abundance of love, warmly expressed from the moment he is put to his mother's breast. For mother and child this nursing of her child is important psychologically. I watched Sumiko often as, the third day past, she held him to her breast. The hours were unscheduled.

"He knows when he is hungry," she said.

"How long will you nurse him?" I asked.

"As long as I can," she replied. "I hope until the next child is conceived."

Is Sumiko old-fashioned? Perhaps, for I am told that the youngest mothers now are urged to shorten the period of breast feeding. Sumiko's baby son is fortunate, perhaps. Mother and child lived closely at home until the first month was over, and then he was presented to the family shrine so that his soul would be secure in his body. Thereafter he took a surprisingly lively share in the family life, in his mother's arms or strapped on her back. Wherever she went she took the baby with her and when he was only four months old she began his toilet training, coaxing him by her soft whistling, the same sound I used to hear from Chinese mothers long ago.

Meanwhile the training of the older children went on, gently but continuously, and mainly by example.

"See," Sumiko would say to her elder son. "Your father does not cry when he has work to do. He is a big man."

"I am big, too," the son declared, and immediately became heroic.

Rewards were frequent, a bit of candy bestowed at the right moment, an inexpensive toy. I was interested to observe how both Hideki and Sumiko directed their discipline to prepare a child for his next experience. The little girl, for example, indulged in an occasional tantrum. She was coaxed and teased out of it but with love and patience. As the time came for her to enter school, however, discipline became firmer. She was told that when school began, tantrums must cease or the family would be shamed. To bring shame to the family is the greatest shame for a child. The older son, I remember, was taken to a Buddhist priest before he went to school, in order to "cure" him of not wanting to get up in the morning. I do not know exactly how the priest treated this particular ailment, but priestly healing in Japan usually takes the form of a serious discussion between priest and child, a private prayer by the priest, and the subsequent pronouncement of cure. Sometimes, if the child's naughtiness has been particularly severe, more drastic measures may be taken. Then a small pile of moxa, a powdered medicinal herb, is placed on the skin and ignited. The burn leaves its mark on the skin and the mind, and is usually most effective in curing such parental complaints as childish tantrums and obstinacy. The treatment sounds perhaps extreme, but the burn is small though sharp, and seldom needs to be repeated.

Discipline for the Matsumoto children, as for all Japanese youngsters, applied even to sleep. Sumiko taught her little daughter to lie straight at night, her legs together, and to be quiet. Her son had more freedom, yet he too could not disturb his quilts without his mother's gentle remarks of praise for his father and for his uncle, her own brother, whom the child loved. By emulation of some admirable and admired man the little boy's standards were set.

Yet this same loving family can turn hard-hearted and reject a son when he is obdurate and will not learn. I say son, for I have not heard of a Japanese girl who refused discipline. But Sumiko told me of Hideki's youngest brother, who was troublesome at home and idle in school, to the point where he was considered by all to be shaming his family. At the age of ten he was rejected by family and teachers alike, and even by his schoolmates, so that he had nowhere to go. He lived in an empty shack near his parents' house and his mother took him food until she could arrange for his return through mediation with the family. He came back a humbled child, and they had no more difficulty with him. He had learned what it was to be cast out from his sole security, his family. It was a bitter lesson but it taught a truth about life in Japan, that the individual is lost without his family.

What is the secret of the Japanese teaching of self-discipline? It lies, I think, in the fact that the aim of all teaching is the establishment of habit. Rules are repeated over and over, and continually practiced until obedience becomes instinctive. This repetition is enhanced by the expectation of the elders. They expect a child to obey and to learn through obedience. The demand is gentle at first and tempered to the child's tender age. It is no less gentle as time goes on, but certainly it is increasingly inexorable. Hideki, discussing the technique one day, said of his own childhood, "I felt as though I were enveloped in a soft net that clung to me wherever I went. I was free to come and go, since I was a boy, yet wherever I went there was some sort of pressure on me, gentle and relentless at the same time. It was the high expectations of my family, weaving around me."

"But will you and Sumiko weave the same web about your children?" I asked.

"No," he said. He paused to consider and then repeated the word firmly. "No, we will not."

But Sumiko, listening, was silent.

Now, far away from that warm Japanese house, I reflect upon what I learned there. What, I wonder, will take the place of that web of love and discipline which for so many centuries has surrounded the life and thinking of the people of Japan? For freedom can be a frightening atmosphere in which to live. I watched upon the television screen not long ago the image of an astronaut floating free in space, tethered only by a single life line, and somehow was reminded of the peoples on this earth who today are repeating the experience, only not in physical space. The peoples of India, Indonesia and Indochina were once secure in the often uncomfortable but nevertheless responsible keeping of foreign imperial rule. In prewar India, for example, young people complained that they could do nothing because the British ruled, but I observed a certain insouciance, a shrugging off of responsibility that at times was almost gay. A recent postwar visit to India, however, revealed a very different people. Insouciance had changed to a worried air of responsibility, and self-criticism was healthy and strong. In Japan, too, I see the same change. True, there have been no foreign rulers in that country against whom to revolt, but there has been the web of a traditional government and society. Each people of course has today as valid a life line as the astronaut, provided they cling to it as he did. The people of Japan have their life line in a selective preservation of such traditions as will serve them in our modern times.

The traditions most likely to serve are, I believe, those based upon what the Japanese call "human feelings," not all of which have anything to do with the pursuit of pleasure. MacArthur, for example, was making use of "human feelings" when, following the directive from Washington, he maintained the position of the emperor. The people of Japan would have felt lost had the basic structure of their traditional government, centering about the emperor, been destroyed. Their most profound "human feelings" would have been shattered without remedy. No one knows this better than the Japanese people themselves. Indeed, in her victorious war with Russia, Japan used the same successful consideration as a conqueror. When General Stoessel, the Russian commander, declared himself ready to surrender, this at Port Arthur in 1905, General Nogi of Japan clasped Stoessel's hand and praised his leadership of the courageous Russian defense. Stoessel, much touched, expressed his regret over the loss of Nogi's two sons in the war and then, in supreme sacrifice, he gave his favorite white horse to the conqueror. General Nogi replied by saying that he must give the horse to the emperor, but if it was returned to him, he would care for it as long as it lived. The horse was returned to General Nogi, and he built a stable as handsome as a shrine near his own house and cared for the horse as scrupulously as he had promised to do. Thus he acted in accordance with "human feelings."

There is a contrast, I admit, between the attitude in Japan toward "human feelings" and the severe repression of the individual. Yet I doubt that "contrast" is the word. I say rather that consideration of "human feelings" provides an outlet for the repressed individual. It is inevitable that the weight of obligation upon the individual at times becomes unbearable and outbreak takes place. Judgment is not as severe as it might be upon such occasions, for "human feelings" offer atonement. I am reminded at this moment of my friends the Yamaguchi family, the name disguised, of course. Mr. Yamaguchi is one of the great financiers and businessmen of Japan. He has a younger son, let us call him Isamu, who has been a source of worry to him. Isamu is a modern young man. He has twenty-five Western suits, three cars and an unquenchable hatred of school. Some years ago Mr. Yamaguchi asked me to see that Isamu entered an American college. It would be better, the father felt, for the son to get away from his night-club companions in Tokyo. The season was late, colleges were filled, but finally I succeeded in entering him in a midwestern college. In a short time I began to get letters from the dean. It seemed that Isamu did not consider it necessary to get out of bed in the morning in order to go to classes. He was not accustomed to it. Also he considered it beneath his dignity to take examinations. In short, it appeared that he was living in Ohio exactly as he had in Japan. Moreover, he had already accumulated a group of friends, through his charm and with the help of ample funds.

"Isamu has far too much money," the troubled dean wrote me. "He has at least five hundred dollars a month."

I promised to try to reason with Isamu when he spent his Christmas vacation with us. I was somewhat discouraged, however, after he appeared at my home. He was a large amiable young man, compliant and smiling. My three youngest adopted daughters, themselves half-Japanese, took him over and teased him without mercy. He was unruffled, immovable, unchangeable. I began to understand the dean's complaints. Yet Isamu was never a trouble. He made no demands, he ate anything, he joined in our family life if he wished, or he withdrew to his room to sleep. When, as usual, we went to Vermont for skiing after Christmas, he accompanied us, and bought an expensive and elaborate outfit. Looking like a solemn owl in his snow goggles, he skied when he felt like it and when he did not he stayed at home and slept. At the end of his vacation he returned to college unregenerated. I simply had not felt able to talk to him. What could I say? He was as he was. At the end of the school year he announced that he would return to Japan. His agitated father refused to send money for his ticket and offered instead to buy him a Lincoln Continental with which to tour the United States. Isamu said he would drive to California, sell the car and come home.

Two years later he suddenly appeared at my New York apartment, bringing me a gift from his parents. I asked him what he was doing back in the United States. He said he was studying industrial design in order to help his father in the family business. I saw, in fact, a young man completely reformed, regenerate and serious. The web had enveloped him, as it had enveloped my other young friend Wasaburo, and he was functioning within its containment. Yet when I asked him where he was living, he replied with a smile that he had an apartment in Greenwich Village, which place he found almost as amusing as certain parts of Tokyo. I offered to introduce him to some young Americans, since he might be lonely. To this he replied simply, "Thank you, I already have too many friends."

My last letter from Mr. Yamaguchi was in the summer. He had heard a rumor that I was coming to Japan and if it was true, I must let him know. Isamu was ready to drive me anywhere in his new Mercedes, a prospect that I found quite terrifying.

"You will like to know," Mr. Yamaguchi wrote, "Isamu is now a very good son. He helps me very much in business. We are thinking to marry him to my friend's daughter."

Yes, Isamu is in the web. But I know him well enough to know, too, for I did see him again, that at certain times and in certain places he is still very busy with "human feelings."

The web, of course, is not only familial. Mr. Yamaguchi, as a businessman, has his own traditional security. He expects and gets total obedience from his own employees, for example. They follow that part of the web called *bushido,* whereby loyalty gets its reward in the certainties of seniority. Modern as Mr. Yamaguchi is, his plant up to the highest American standards, in spirit he is a daimyo merchant, an overlord over his samurai employees. They will serve him without question because it is good personal relations. Mr. Yamaguchi follows the same good relations with his equals in business, rejecting excessive competition with them in consideration of "human feelings." To force a competitor to fail in business would be as unhappy an experience for Mr. Yamaguchi as to fail himself. The Japanese businessman believes in cooperation rather than competition and Mr. Yamaguchi belongs to an association of business firms like his own, where prices and distribution are discussed and agreed upon.

Within his own offices Mr. Yamaguchi observes a ritual. He does not like young men who are too bright and ambitious and to that extent he approves of Isamu. He disapproves mainly because his son did not graduate from the proper schools. Nevertheless he is proud that his own brother, Isamu's uncle, is a member of the Diet. It is a compensating fact. Still, he would have liked Isamu to be one of the two thousand graduates from Tokyo University. Even an American degree is secondary. But he accepts his son now, degreeless as he is.

As for Isamu, he seems entirely happy. He has a flexible expense account, as all Japanese businessmen have, and it allows him ample entertainment at night clubs and bars, where he meets other young businessmen. One of his obligations is to represent his father in meeting American businessmen and guiding them to such places of amusement. He uses considerable skill in this sort of thing and often entices American customers from other companies by the magnificence of his gifts. Here "human feelings" take over. The American in a strange country is usually as inhibited as any Japanese. After a mellowing amount of liquor, however, and the attentions of pretty hostesses, both men reach the same level of "human feelings," and recognizing their similar state, are able to do business.

Mr. Yamaguchi is traditional, of course. He expects lifelong loyalty from his employees. They have been carefully chosen as to family and education after recommendation by friends and relatives known to Mr. Yamaguchi; and so long as they make the company their life, and he their industrial absolute ruler, he will provide security until death. The bond is mutual. He would no more think of firing a loyal and competent employee than the latter would think of leaving him. What Mr. Yamaguchi does not know, however, is that his son Isamu, looking toward the future, is questioning the web. Perhaps his stay in the United States brought some change in his private soul. At least I caught a glimpse of it on my last day in Tokyo, when we were driving—yes, in the Mercedes—to see a friend in Oiso.

"So some day you will be the head of Yamaguchi Industries," I remarked. "It is an empire, isn't it?"

Isamu speeded up another ten miles an hour. He spoke out of the wind. "I shall not rule as my father does. He is really quite feudal. I shall employ men on their own merits. I think it is better."

Isamu will not be alone in this decision. Some Japanese companies are already moving in the direction of American business and are hiring men on ability rather than family connections. To this extent the ancient rule is giving way to modern freedom.

IX

THE SOFT WEB enveloping the Japanese child becomes a tightly drawn net for the adult. It is not always an unwelcome net, for it offers a security that only rules, always obeyed, can give, but it is inexorable. "Discipline," "duty," "obligation" are key words in Japanese life. There is a time to be guided by "obligation" and a time to be guided by "human feelings," but where there is a conflict between the two there is only one proper choice. Youthful waywardness is forgiven, yes; but only so far and no further. At times the conflicts between doing what one has to do because it is required and doing what one wants to do because it is desirable, or even just and merciful, can be severe. Yet honor, the fulfillment of duty, must always be satisfied. Self-indulgence must never be allowed when its result is shame. There is shame in placing oneself in an awkward position; shame in failure; shame in humiliating another; shame in miscalculating the exact amount of respect due to people on various levels of society. Obligations, which are countless, must be met promptly and fully. Sometimes there is only one way to fulfill an obligation, to save oneself from shame through failure to do the proper thing at the proper time and in the proper place, and that is death. Throughout Japanese history the samurai committed suicide because of *giri,* and though the samurai have gone, giri remains.

What is giri? If pressed into Western terminology, giri is a moral imperative, a spiritual obligation which, if it cannot otherwise be paid in full, must be fulfilled by destroying one's life. Perhaps it is best expressed by the old French phrase *noblesse oblige.* Or, if one is to use the words of a Japanese dictionary, "giri is the righteous way, the road human beings should follow; something one does, though unwillingly, to forestall apology to the world." Giri relationships are those a man has toward his family, his in-laws, to those above him in station and government, and to those beneath him who are dependent on him. It has to do with one's personal honor in all relationships; it has to do with "clearing one's name," with "keeping one's proper place," with paying debts and reciprocating gifts and kindnesses, indeed, with virtually every area of Japanese life.

The effect is a heavy and permanent burden on Japanese shoulders, for it is never possible to work off all the giri obligations that accumulate in the course of daily living. The smallest favor, even the offer of a cigarette or a glass of water, demands reciprocation. Because each gift, favor, or word of praise must, in effect, be paid for, the Japanese will often go out of their way to avoid being recipients. They are actually resentful of casual favors or compliments offered by strangers, for they have enough obligations toward their relatives and acquaintances without having to take on obligations thrust upon them by outsiders. So resentful are they of incurring unwanted obligations that they have developed strange ways of saying thank you. In Japanese there is no direct way of saying this simple phrase. Instead they use words and phrases that translate into such expressions of regret, indeed, of rancor, as: "It is unrepayable," "Oh, this difficult thing!" "I am insulted, I am grateful," "This unextinguishable debt!" "Oh, this poisonous feeling!" And it must be a poisonous feeling, to be eternally indebted to practically every acquaintance.

Partly because of their fear of becoming obligated or imposing obligation upon another, which could start a cycle that might be never-ending, and partly because of their feeling about Fate, the Japanese tend to be even less interested in getting involved with other people's problems than are Westerners. To involve oneself in any problem situation is to take the risk of failing and being criticized, or of performing a deed which will involve the doer too deeply for comfort in a new web of mutual obligation. This deliberate avoidance of involvement makes the Japanese appear unfeeling and cruel, indifferent to the sufferings of others. In effect, because of their code of behavior, they are. But so far as their human feelings are concerned, they are by no means cruel and indifferent. They are caught in the web of giri and Fate.

It is also a fact that the whole idea of human involvement is foreign to Asia. I do not, for instance, think that an Asian country would think of sending food to starving nations, to another country. For all our faults, and for all that we may hope for in return, we Americans do, and I hope that in this respect we will never change. This reaching out and helping other peoples is, I think, a light in the world. But Asians feel that it is not for man to serve in this way. If Fate, or Heaven, sends a famine or some other disaster, why should the victims be helped, why send rescue? To do so would be to defy the gods. They feel much the same way about disasters that afflict their own people and their own country. Nowadays the government and the Japanese Red Cross do lend a hand in case of such national tragedy as earthquake or typhoon, but the Japanese people themselves are not oriented toward the lending of a helping hand. Fate has decreed. Who is man to interfere? Until government and organizational aid came into existence, only the Buddhists could be expected to offer any assistance, and they did so not for the sake of humanity but because it was a good deed and would help them on their way to heaven. Asian people regard this as an understandable and even worthy aim.

There is a story that I have told before, but I tell it again to illustrate the point. Though it happened in China it might have happened anywhere in Asia. It did happen in China because that is where my father was. My father was inclined sometimes to preach a little too long. One day he was preaching in a Chinese church, where the people do not sit quietly and rest but get up and walk around if they are bored, and even chat to each other to pass the time. On this day my father's sermon was long and people began to get up and go about their business. My father went on preaching and the people went on chatting and wandering around. An old woman in a front seat called out, "Sit down, sit down! Can't you see he's working his way to heaven?"

This personal attitude of helpfulness is expressed in other ways as well. In Japan, though there is no feeling of responsibility among individuals to open their arms and homes to strangers when disaster strikes, there is a feeling of neighborliness. In a neighbor's time of need there may be a bond of friendship as strong as a blood tie. I myself have had the most touching exhibitions of this, when, in time of trouble, a friend has come to the rescue and has literally given everything. Friends do open arms and homes and hearts when they are needed.

But it is seldom that they rush to the rescue of strangers, though even here there are exceptions. Japanese life is full of exceptions and contradictions, and to generalize is perhaps unfair. Yet it is true that the Japanese people often seem almost cruel in their rejection of a kind act. If a stranger suffers an accident in the street, or falls into the water and cannot swim, or screams for assistance because his house is on fire, the average Japanese will not help. No, he leaves his victim to his Fate. The hurt, the drowning, the loss, are all ordained by the gods, and to rush in is not only to interfere with destiny but to expose oneself to the risk of a new obligation cycle.

One great exception to this is the Japanese attitude immediately following the atomic blasts at Hiroshima and Nagasaki. At that time there were many examples of individual heroism and self-sacrifice, particularly among the priests and ministers. I know of several cases where people happened to be out in the country when the horror occurred, and hurried back to the disaster area to do everything possible to help, and many other cases, too, where individuals, themselves bereft and in pain, risked their lives for others. For their families, yes, for friends, yes, but for strangers also. At the same time there were many who did sit back and do nothing. For them, again, it was Fate.

The war was a time of great personal conflict for many Japanese who had been conditioned by the giri convention to do their duty and yet could not disregard their human feelings. Giri to his emperor and his commander would compel a man to kill, though often he did not want to. Of course he did kill. His obligation to his leaders was greater than all others. But there were many times when the individual Japanese would deny his giri and spare his American opponent, even helping him to escape. Militarists apart, the Japanese people did not want war, and though the majority of them fought with fervor for their divine emperor there were many who could not reconcile duty with the feelings of the heart. Even in the face of centuries of tradition, and the great feeling of guilt and failure that comes with the denial of giri, they were swayed by human feelings. The savagery and suicidal courage of other Japanese fighting men can be explained in terms of their total commitment to their emperor-god, to whom they owed their greatest obligation, and their belief that they themselves would be deified in death. Those who failed their emperor by being cornered or captured fulfilled their obligation by killing themselves. For bushido, the code of the samurai, made such a debt extinguishable only in the destruction of self.

Suicide is still considered the perfect solution for a debt unpaid, for perfection unachieved. Fortunately the Japanese of today are less determined than before to search out the perfect solution to compensate for their failure to pay their various debts. If a businessman, for example, is unable to pay his financial debts within the specified time, he no longer commits suicide in place of payment. Instead, he asks for an extension. Practical creditors approve of this change. Giri suicide is still acceptable repayment in the light of tradition, but from the point of view of paying the rent it is far from satisfactory.

Hara-kiri, more politely known as *seppuku,* is no longer often practiced, since the sword went out with the samurai. But Japan's suicide rate is still high, indicating that solution by death has not altogether lost its appeal. On the southern coast of Hokkaido there is a spa called Noboribetsu where one may find the greatest collection of volcanic craters and scalding springs in all Japan. In a strange dark valley, called the Valley of Hell or sometimes Grand Hell, wreaths and curls of white smoke emerge from the barren earth. From a point above one may look down into two boiling hot lakes, one large, one small. In the spring a dismaying number of Japanese commit suicide by leaping into the smaller of the boiling lakes. Spring is the favored time, and craters still hold much of their morbid charm. But today any Japanese bent on killing himself is just as likely to throw himself under the wheels of the Tokaido Super Express or take an overdose of pills. And the main reason for suicide is not love or giri. It is weariness with life; it is neurosis.

Of course it may still have something to do with giri and the weighty obligations it imposes. It is easy to understand that life for the Japanese, bound with restrictions as it is, may become tiring. Even genuinely kindly and spontaneous acts of generosity carry their weight and their sting.

For instance, the Japanese are great gift givers. This is a habit that stems partly from genuine warmth and partly from custom. There is no occasion when a gift is not appropriate, and no day when there is no occasion. This, too, is something that becomes part of the Japanese nature in early childhood, and it can be a very warm and endearing thing. Japanese children love to exchange gifts. They may not at first understand that giri requires them to match a gift received with a return gift of their own, but they early become accustomed to the delights of giving and receiving. A friend of mine, an American actress, told me an illuminating little tale some months ago about her small daughter. My friend spends much of her time in Hollywood but she has a home in Japan where her husband, also an American, is a film producer, and she commutes between her Japanese home and the United States. The little daughter is being educated in Japan, but she too comes over to this country quite often when her mother is working on a picture and spends some time in her American home. This child, her mother told me, was so used to giving gifts to her small friends in Japan that she carried the custom over into this country. No doubt her new American friends were delighted to receive her presents, but they did not know the rules. So the child was deeply hurt when the American children gave her nothing in return, after she had given away practically everything she had. She reported this to her mother. "But, Mother," she said plaintively, "they don't give *me* anything!"

In Japan they would have. For in Japan one must reciprocate a gift. One usually wants to, but one always has to. Like so many other obligations, this one also causes difficulties. If the return gift is perhaps not as good as the one received, it is thought to have some ominous significance. If it is very much better, then the recipient is likely to feel that his gift was not good enough. Then both are in the wrong: the donor for being ostentatious and putting his friend to shame, and the recipient for having given a gift that clearly was inadequate. He, then, will reply with another gift, and his friend is obliged to reciprocate. Even if the gifts are absolutely equal the exchange must be kept up. Often a cycle that started with a small spontaneous gift is carried to ludicrous extremes and may only end with the death of one of the parties. Even then it is entirely possible that the relatives of the deceased may feel obliged to take over. The whole business of gift-giving thus becomes highly artificial and loses all its human value, unless of course the exchange is carried on judiciously by close friends who know each other's tastes and make each offering as a sign of affection. This does happen, of course, but more often there is a sort of desperation in both the choosing and giving of gifts, and the cycle becomes painfully formalized and presents something of the aspects of a duel. It is not uncommon, especially among poorer people, for one of the gift givers to go into debt in trying to keep up his end of the exchange. In a way, this is typical of giri: in avoiding shame by fulfilling obligations, one pays a heavy price. In this, as in other areas of Japanese life, the toll on human feelings comes very high.

The Japanese realize this and have always realized it. Yet the system of obligation and reciprocation, despite the resentments it breeds, has changed little in Japan. It, too, is a web that envelops the Japanese people, and its main strands are obligations to family, parents, and emperor. It has never been broken. It is true that with the war's end for a while everything time-honored was rejected impulsively, including the old family system that is so closely tied to duty and obligation. But rejection was not incisive, and beneath the surface of rebellious confusion the old ways still waited, intact. Now, after twenty years, much of patriarchy and filial piety has returned, and most of the old and the young do put the demands of giri, particularly in respect to the family, ahead of the desires of the individual. The demands of the family, the class, the community and the nation take precedence, and the Japanese think this is right. Perhaps it is. Certainly this philosophy in practice is a unifying force in a nation that is changing in so many surface ways.

How DOES the emperor of Japan view the changes in his domain? When I was in Kyushu I was invited to be one of a group to welcome His Imperial Majesty and the Empress when their private train arrived at Fukuoka. The imperial pair were making a visit to the island and began their tour at this ancient city. I stood in the forefront of the crowd with representatives from the diplomatic corps. At a shout, prearranged, we all bowed deeply. My only view of Their Majesties at first was of their two pairs of feet, plodding courageously but somewhat wearily along the cement platform of the station. Recovering from the bow, again at a given signal, I saw a middle-aged man in a business suit, and some distance behind him, in the proper position for a woman, albeit an empress, a middle-aged lady in a long, old-fashioned Western dress and big hat. He was serious and abstracted, or so I thought, but she was smiling shyly and even anxiously. The crowd, however, maintained its reverent attitude until Their Imperial Majesties were out of sight. I was compelled to believe that the reluctant occupant of the

Chrysanthemum Throne is as widely revered and respected as ever.

This thirty-ninth year of Showa finds the Japanese imperial system remodeled and reformed, but it is still intact and unchallenged, although it is true that times themselves have changed. Now the Emperor, accompanied by the Empress, makes frequent trips up and down the country with a minimum of formality. Guest lists at imperial garden parties held each autumn embrace a wide cross-section of people, including the foreign press. And twice every year, on January 2 and April 29, the gates of the Imperial Palace inner grounds are thrown open to admit all desiring to greet the Emperor at the New Year or on his birthday. So after two decades of democratization of one of the oldest thrones on earth, emperor and people are united by close bonds of sentiment, tradition, and mutual regard and respect. In the warmer relationship of today there is less remoteness on the one hand and slightly less awe on the other. Not long ago at Hayama Beach, where Their Imperial Majesties maintain a villa, visitors heard a loudspeaker voice politely imploring bathers to "please get off the Emperor's boat." People were using it for a diving platform! Now this would have been unthinkable in former times, when anything even remotely connected with the emperor would have been considered sacred.

Times indeed have changed, and for the better, I think, so far as the imperial family are concerned, for their lives are certainly less lonely than they used to be in the centuries of isolated grandeur. It is better to be loved than feared. Yet I am warned by Japanese friends that reverence for authority and status are re-emerging in Japan, for the people are still very ritual-minded. It may be true, therefore, as some say, that little by little the emperor is being pulled back into seclusion. But it is still a long, long way back to the time when the 124th descendant of Jimmu was "divine."

X

HOW DO Americans fare in Japan, now that the occupation is over? It depends on what they are doing there. Guests are royally treated, visitors are welcome, tourists are well served. An American teacher says, "For me the problems are few, the rewards great." But other people, businessmen in particular, are not always so happy. The difficulty of communication between our countries that was a major cause of estrangement continues today, though we are no longer enemies. Language is a great obstacle. Translators, as often as not, serve to aggravate rather than ease this difficulty. The tendency of the interpreter is to pretend to understand, out of politeness or pride or both, when actually he has not fully understood what was said. Interpreters sometimes even embroider the facts or substitute fabrications of their own if they feel that the original speech was lacking in what they think ought to have been said. Japanese businessmen may themselves pretend to understand when they do not. Businessmen, therefore, are often working in some degree of darkness.

Attempts to learn the other's language are enormously time-consuming and frustrating for both Americans and Japanese. Our languages are too different for either of us to acquire any real fluency in the other's tongue. Ours is based on an alphabet, only mildly phonetic. Theirs is based on Chinese and Chinese ideographs, simplified by their own phonetics. It must be said that among the many talents of the Japanese, linguistic ability is not included. Most Americans suffer from the same lack, especially in regard to Asian tongues and most particularly in the extremely difficult language of the Japanese. Of the two peoples, the Japanese are under the greatest linguistic disadvantage. Generally speaking, among all the Asian peoples the Japanese seem to have the greatest difficulty with foreign languages, perhaps particularly with English. Their own complex language is a handicap to the understanding of others.

A Japanese today has three languages to learn, all his own. The first is Kanji, written in ideographic script based on Chinese but adapted for Japanese use, so that it is as different from the original form as English is different from Latin. There are thousands of Kanji ideographs, and one needs a knowledge of about 2,000 of them to read the newspaper. The second is kana, a phonetic syllabary of about a hundred letter sounds. This is a shortened script, still similar to Chinese ideographs but much abbreviated. It may be written either in *katakana,* the square characters, or *hiragana,* the cursive characters. The third is the Japanese modification of English, as for example *mobo* for "modern boy," *chiiko dansu* for "cheek-to-cheek-dancing," *pi-chi-ay* for P.T.A., *esukareita* for "escalator," *aisukurima* for "ice cream," *basuboru* for "baseball," *amachua* for "amateur," *biru* for "beer," and so on into the hundreds of words. In none of the three languages is there a distinction between *r* and *l,* a fatal fault in learning English, where they are two important consonants. In addition to their three "languages," the Japanese have to master *romaji,* Japanese spelled in Roman letters. It is thus difficult enough for the Japanese to learn all forms of his own language without having to learn English, and extremely difficult for a Westerner to learn Japanese.

In syntax and grammar, too, we have nothing in common. Japanese philologists classify the parts of speech quite differently from the way we do. They maintain four basic parts of speech: substantives, conjugatives, modifiers and particles. Prefixes, suffixes and honorifics are numerous, each with its own significance in place, time, and human relationship. In Japanese the English pronoun "I," for instance, has twenty equivalents; none of them are interchangeable, and each may be used only in certain circumstances. Verbs are wanton in their variety, although they have neither person nor number. They are lacking in time sense, but fraught with mood sense—potential, optative, prohibitive and negative.

But even for Japanese and American to learn the other's language is not enough to ensure communication of ideas. The American in Japan must put aside his habits of precision, brevity, extroversion. He must assume the Japanese mood of subjectivity, timelessness, universality. He must accept the fact that Japanese is a language of imagination and poesy, not of abstract ideas in science or philosophy. Yet in spite of the inexactness of Japanese expression, the Japanese have been able to achieve astonishing results in modern science. Language sometimes fails them in expressing their findings. But American scientists have the same difficulty in defining the exactitudes of the new physics. The result is that a fresh means of communication has developed, the language of mathematics, in which the Japanese, it appears, can function as nimbly as his Western fellow scientists.

Though the difficulties for them are enormous and their aptitude generally slight, the Japanese make great efforts to learn English. An American in Japan finds himself constantly beset to speak English. The high school boy on the bus will announce with apologetic determination that he will speak with you in English. And before one can say, "Please do," he is off on the phrases he's sure of. He is not being rude when he asks how old one is. This just happens to be one of the few phrases he knows in English. One should answer simply without qualifications, never repeating something in a different way. For example, if one answers, "I'm thirty," well and good. But if one adds, "and I'll be thirty-one next month," the student is lost at once.

An American instructor in English at a Japanese university told me about his experience with this eagerness to learn, commenting thus: "Japanese are ingenious sometimes in getting you involved in conversation so that they can practice speaking and hearing, particularly the latter. One pretty young thing at college came to me in tears one day with a tale of unrequited love. Her story was continued over a whole semester, with me sitting there like a male Ann Landers, giving out with advice to the lovelorn. It turned out to be all a hoax, and probably just as well. I'm sure my advice was very poor. But the young lady accomplished what she set out to do. By the end of the semester she was quite proficient in English and she became an interpreter for the Olympic games. I feel I should at least have got a free ticket!"

It is the rare American who puts so much effort into learning Japanese. This is understandable, since of course Japanese does not have the universality of French or English, and because it is so very difficult. A Westerner may learn the kana characters, with their sounds and meanings. He may learn hundreds, even thousands of Kanji, and he may, after much patient practice, be able to carry on a conversation with his Japanese friends. But unless he is unusually talented he will not be able to understand Japanese people when they talk among themselves. The language is too full of idioms, mood meanings, shortcuts and circumlocutions, euphemisms and different levels of politeness. One who is not born in Japan, one who does not learn Japanese as a child, never attains the fluency of the native speaker.

Language is not the only barrier between American and Japanese. The problem of communication goes beyond words, which can be translated, to ways of thinking, which cannot. Language does, to a great extent, express patterns of thought and ways of thinking, but deeds and practices are even more revelatory. Thus a second difference between our peoples is best expressed perhaps by the Japanese tea ceremony, an indispensable procedure for the refreshment of the Japanese mind and spirit but for most Americans an incomprehensible and puzzling bore. It has been explained many times, but let me try once again. In the first place the ceremony is a rite which may have been begun in ancient times by Buddhist monks, who drank tea to keep themselves awake while they meditated. From the simple business of sipping tea from a bowl the ritual of a series of formal gestures developed with the purpose of cleansing the mind of foolish and irrelevant thoughts and of lifting the spirit out of desperation into calm enlightenment. The ceremony thus helped the individual to attain a control, a self-discipline, a purification which prepared the spirit to receive communication from an object of beauty or a vista of nature. In order that this absolute purity be achieved, the tools and the environment must be in keeping. Therefore, the tea house must be simple and without elaborate decoration. It should be placed in rustic surroundings and the path should be narrow and set with worn and beautiful stones. The house itself should have a small entrance hall, or waiting room, another small room which accommodates the utensils, and finally the ceremonial room itself. *Sukiya,* the name for such a retreat, meant originally Abode of Fantasy. Here the owner sits to meditate, to dream, to contemplate beauty. Instead of going to a museum as his Western counterpart does to enjoy works of art, a concept impossible for a Japanese to accept fully, the Japanese keeps his treasures hidden, to enjoy one by one alone or with a few chosen friends. The Japanese shuns the crowd. He admires austerity, which he associates with true elegance. To the extent that we Americans cannot share this ideal of the Japanese, to the extent that we cannot understand or share in the meaning of the tea ceremony, to that extent our two peoples remain distant, each from the other.

Then, too, there are certain differences in American and Japanese manners that lead to difficulty. First, and most important, are our different methods of greeting. I have seen an American put out his hand enthusiastically on meeting a Japanese, only to wind up striking the new acquaintance on the top of the head as he bows low. And I have seen the reverse, the American bowing, in deference to Japanese custom, and the Japanese using the handshake. It is difficult, and I can only suggest waiting for the other person to make the first move. The fact is that Japanese frown on touching when greeting. The forthright manner of the American is a problem. Japanese try to accept it, but many typical American overtures of friendship, the masculine pat on the back, the arm squeeze, are extremely embarrassing, as are the feminine hug or kiss. Japanese *bow,* that is all. And Americans, I am sure, never will succeed in bowing gracefully. Perhaps it is best for each of us to be natural, for when we try, no matter how sincerely, to adopt the other's custom, we succeed only in being clumsy. In time we will learn how to greet when we meet, and the more we are ourselves, the sooner we will learn.

We have learned much already, both of us, but there is still much to learn. The whole matter of politeness is one that offers puzzles to both sides. In a small, crowded country such as Japan life would be extremely uncomfortable if mutual courtesy were not in practice. The Japanese have a rigid code of etiquette that may seem artificial to foreigners but is actually a formalization of their natural politeness. They have not substituted the form for the reality; they have only codified the reality so as to practice it without fault. That there are faults is because their lives have changed and, so far, their rules have not. Naturally, foreigners and particularly Westerners behave according to completely different standards, and the Japanese are often quite baffled by them. Despite the declarations of many "Westernized" Japanese businessmen to the contrary, most Japanese still regard the frankness of the American as discourtesy.

For centuries the people of Japan have been trained and conditioned to speak vaguely in order to avoid the direct statement that might offend. Any American, therefore, who proceeds at once to the subject in his mind, will find himself in difficulties. In the culture which demands that directness and abruptness be carefully avoided, he must be able to deal with intermediaries and "talk around" his subject. Then, too, it must be remembered that the people of Japan have always been taught to suppress their emotions. This is part of their cult of courtesy. One should not, they believe, lay the burden of one's sadness, for example, upon another, or parade an excess of joy or satisfaction, lest another person less fortunate become aware of his own unhappy state. This suppression of emotion, so logical in its reasons, nevertheless disconcerts the American.

What makes things difficult for the Japanese is that Americans do not have any such rules. They are astonished by the freedom of American manners, and they seldom know what to expect or how to behave. In dealing with each other they know exactly how to act and what forms of address to use, and they know exactly how they will be treated in return. But they do not know what to make of the handshaking, backslapping American. The code of etiquette that was so painstakingly developed throughout the centuries in accordance with their needs took no account of strangers, of visitors from far-off lands. Why should it have? They received no such visitors, by their own choice. Today they try to meet us with their Japanese bows and their semi-American handshakes, and they never quite know if what they are doing is right. Often they seem timid and awkward in their dealings with strangers, and Americans to them seem almost unbearably confident and brash. In a word, rude.

Americans, for their part, are struck by the extreme politeness of the Japanese in certain situations, and astonished by what they think of as incredible rudeness under other circumstances. This is a genuine contradiction, and one that is due not only to the difference in our standards but to the dichotomy of the Japanese nature. Here again he is two people: the formal person, with thoughts of discipline and obligation uppermost; and the informal man with human feelings. It is quite true that the same man who is punctilious in his attitude toward his family, friends and business acquaintances, is indifferent, callous, and often rough when encountering strangers who are likely to remain strangers. This is perfectly proper behavior. Every Japanese accepts that he has a formal and an informal self, and among his own people he knows which self to be on all occasions. Any Westerner who has an opportunity to observe a Japanese acquaintance departing graciously from a meeting and stepping onto a crowded street is astonished by the transformation. The manner of his Japanese friend becomes one of almost savage rudeness. He forces his way through the crowd with an utter disregard for the feelings of others, relentlessly determined to make his train or his purchase or whatever it is

OPPOSITE
Fisherman. Kyushu.

Any industry can be found here; fishermen ply the surrounding seas; Japanese artists and craftsmen are among the world's finest.

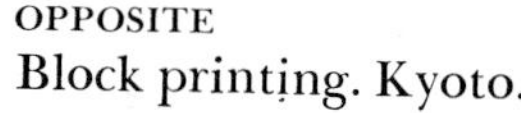

OPPOSITE
Block printing. Kyoto.

Magazine photographer. Tokyo.

Road building. Honshu.

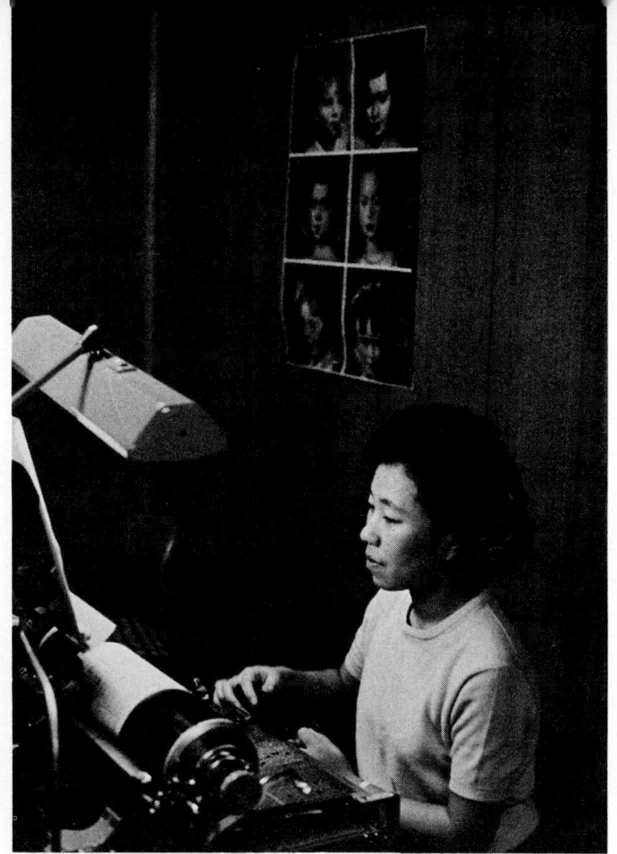

Secretary typing. Tokyo.

Ainu wood carver. Hokkaido.

Early morning fish auction. Tsukiji market, Tokyo.

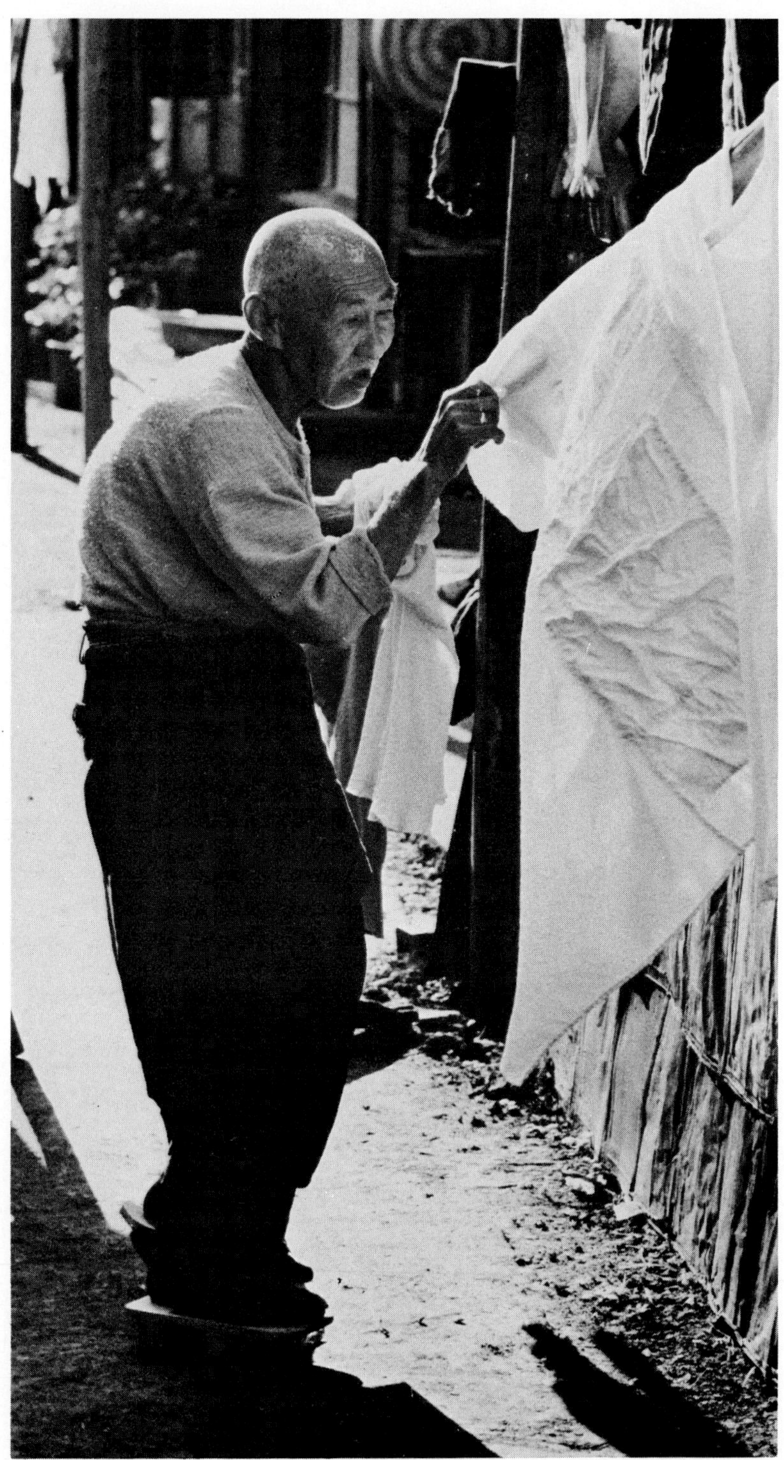

An aged man at the old people's home. Tokyo.

Subway scene. Tokyo.

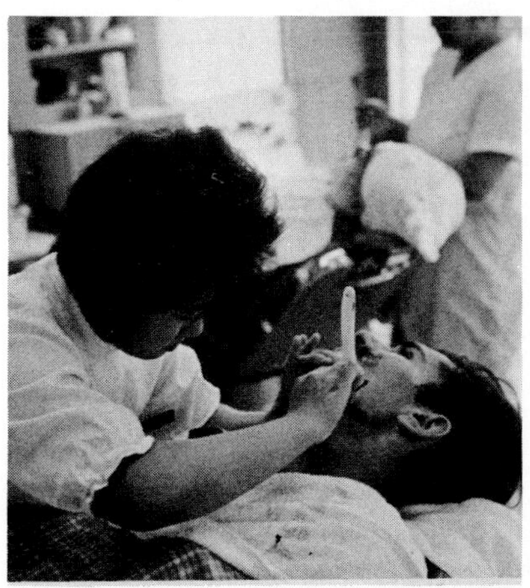

Lady barber. Northern Honshu.

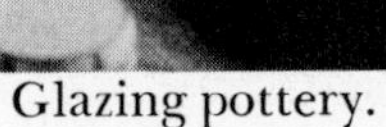

Glazing pottery.

Welder. Honshu.

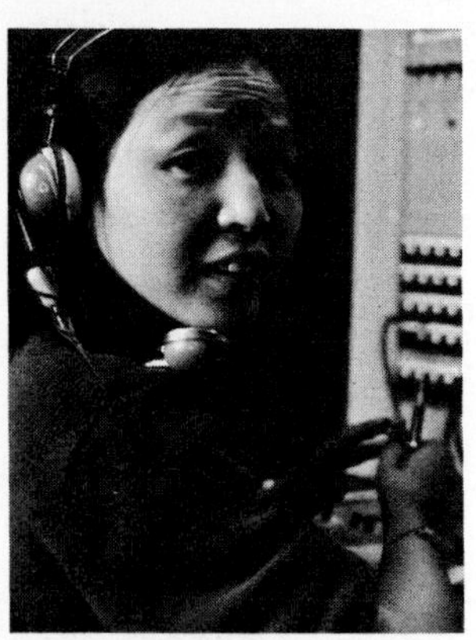

Switchboard operator. Tokyo.

To all their occupations the Japanese bring a grace and skill born of pride and dedication to duty.

Tuna fishermen. Northern Honshu.

Ainu girl dressed for a festival.
Lake Akan, Hokkaido.

And they are pleasure-loving. When work is done they turn to diversion...

Enjoying a game of *Go*. Tokyo.

Children playing.

At a Tokyo restaurant.

Schoolboys playing pool. Tokyo.

Pachinko parlor.

Youths in Harvest Festival procession. Tokyo.

Scuba fishing. Oshima.

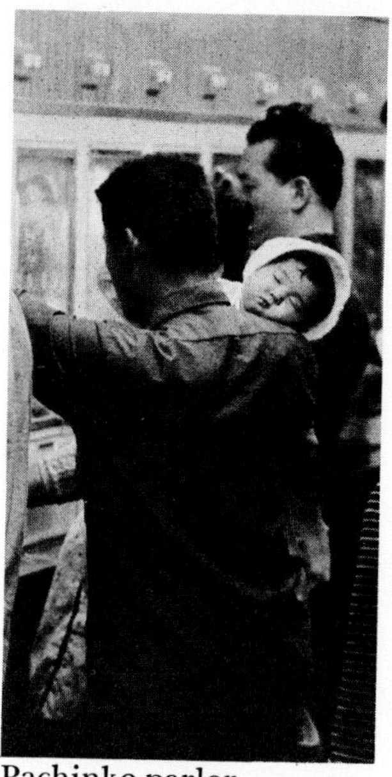
Pachinko parlor.

High school sports exhibition. Tokyo.

...they excel at sports, they delight in festivals and processions. Ever hopeful, they tempt the gods of fortune.

Pause during a hike.
Akan National Park, Hokkaido.

Sukiyaki with entertainment. Tokyo.

Shooting a movie scene. Towa studio.

Nightclub stripper. Tokyo.

They pursue the new "Western-style" entertainment —including the boldest.

Baiko Onoe on stage. *Kabuki* theater, Tokyo.

Theater rehearsal. Tokyo.

And their classical theater flourishes.

Actors on stage. Tokyo.

he is about. The question of offending does not arise. The strangers on the street do not exist for him, any more than he exists for them. It is each man for himself in the anonymous crowd, and the devil take the man whose ribs get in the way of someone else's elbows. But call to your friend as he jostles his way energetically through the other jostlers. He will stop at once, and his manner will again be instantly transformed. Immediately, he is his polite and bowing self, so polite a self, in fact, that he will even push and shove for you.

The Japanese treatment of women is another cause of astonishment for Americans. Courteous though the Japanese may be in the home to his wife and other female members of the household, in public he seems boorish toward all women and even his own wife. It is not for him to open a door and step aside to let a lady walk ahead, nor to help with a coat and guide her into a chair. No, he races her for a seat in the streetcar, and she lets him win. More, even an old woman will give up her seat to a man, so conditioned is she by years of submission. Americans find it extraordinary that women accept this without question. True, there is less acceptance these days, for the American male of occupation days showed eye-opening courtesies to the Japanese woman, and she will never quite forget. But she still allows her men to reserve their courtesies for one another and treat her as a lesser being. The Japanese attitude toward women and strangers is not, so far as they are concerned, rudeness, any more than frankness is rudeness in the American. Both peoples have their customs. And customs of this sort are a persistent barrier. Communication fails when viewpoints differ.

Yet the explanation for failure to communicate may be even more simple. A Japanese man generally feels somewhat ill at ease at first with any foreigner, and the more friendly the foreigner becomes, the more reserved and noncommittal the Japanese becomes. I suppose that the basic emotion is the deep fear, ingrained in the Japanese for centuries, of shaming himself or others. To be shamed is perhaps the greatest evil that can befall a Japanese businessman, and to bring shame or embarrassment to another is almost as great. The only safety, in Japanese tradition and opinion, is to act within the established code of manners and obligations, based on class and position, the ultimate aim being always to accomplish one's plans without bringing embarrassment or dishonor to oneself or to others. Indeed, in Japanese opinion, the two are the same, since to shame another person is to shame oneself.

XI

SINCE HONOR and obligation to others are sacred, so to speak, to the people of Japan, it may be inquired if they are a religious people. It would appear that they are not.

At present, despite centuries of Buddhist and Shinto rituals, probably seventy per cent of the people, ninety per cent of the young, are agnostic and careless of theories of future life. They live in the present and in the hope of better living upon earth. They have no faith, or very little, in anything beyond their own abounding vitality. Death they accept as inevitable in the end and as possible at any moment on their storm-racked islands. There is an effect, even upon their vitality, of this constant presence of catastrophe. It may be said that Japan is a death-oriented country, and America a life-oriented one, that Japanese are pessimistic, Americans optimistic. It is the optimism of Christians that Japanese find difficult to accept. Indeed, there is comparatively little acceptance of Christianity among them.

Among the various religions of Japan perhaps Shintoism has had the greatest influence, even though in recent years, since the withdrawal of government support, there has been a decline. The word "Shinto" comes from two Chinese words, *shen* and *tao,* which may be translated as "God Lore." Shintoism is a combination of love of gods, love of earth and love of country. Through this trinity it has reached into every area of Japanese life, and was indeed used by government for military and nationalistic purposes.

In his book *Japan, Past and Present* Harvard Professor Edwin O. Reischauer, a long-time resident and student of Japan, says: "Shinto was based on a simple feeling of awe in the presence of any surprising or awesome phenomenon of nature—a waterfall, a mountain crag, a large tree, a peculiarly shaped stone, or even some lowly thing awesome only in its capacity for irritation, such as an insect. Anything awe-inspiring was called *kami,* a word usually translated as 'god' but basically meaning 'above,' and by extension 'superior.' This simple concept of deity should be borne in mind in trying to understand the deification in modern Japan of living Emperors and of all Japanese soldiers who have died for their country."

In *All the Best in Japan,* Sydney Clark quotes a Japanese scholar, J. Tabaku: "Shintoism is not to be considered a religion and its spirits are by no means gods. Shinto is a composite of old beliefs, customs, good luck omens, and national ritual. Its only purpose is to develop loyalty to one's land, one's long-established way of life."

So speaks a modern and agnostic Japanese. As a matter of fact, Shintoism has had two aspects, the first before 1945 and the second after that date. Until the end of the war it was a state institution, a national faith based on belief in the divinity of the emperor as the true descendant of the sun-goddess. Sophisticated Japanese statesmen of Meiji times had made use of an ancient cult, based on a people's awe of nature in islands, perhaps the most spectacularly beautiful and dangerous in the whole world, to consolidate the emperor's position and their own. They played upon the awe that was expressed through a belief that spirits dwell in rain and wind, sea and mountain, and succeeded in extending its area to include what was awesome in national and political life. In order that the adherents of other religions could take part in it, they declared Shintoism to be no more than "a sign of respect toward civil institutions," but a sign of respect that everyone was to show. Not to show it was to fail in one's duty to exalted national symbols such as the emperor. Thus, from the Meiji era until World War II, Japanese statesmen stressed the deification of the emperor for their own purposes, and succeeded in developing Japanese nationalism to an extraordinary degree. At the end of the war the emperor destroyed the chief foundation of post-Meiji Shintoism by disavowing his own divinity. A further blow was the abolition of official financial support for Shinto shrines and ceremonies, and the shrines fell into disuse. Shintoism was, in effect, denationalized and discredited. It has revived somewhat during the years of peace and some of the more appealing of the old ceremonies are still practiced. Shrines have been repaired and people visit them. But today Shintoism is generally accepted to be a tradition rather than a religion, "a composite of old beliefs," and State Shintoism is a thing of the past.

There is and always has been a tremendous contrast between the primitive cult of Shintoism and the profound, rich and sophisticated religion of Buddhism. To neither Buddhist nor Shintoist was it odd that the two could exist side by side, nor that a man could believe in both doctrines although they flatly contradicted each other. Japanese accept the contradictions within themselves, difficult though this may sometimes be for us.

Japan accepted the India-oriented religion of Buddhism only upon her own terms, and the form most developed by Japanese character and tradition is that known as Zen. Like other schools of Buddhism, Zen teaches that one can only understand the universe by overcoming all the illusions of life, whether in being or non-being. The difference between Zen and other forms of Buddhism, however, is that Zen rejects all intellectualism and relies wholly on intuition. Enlightenment does not, it claims, come about through long study but in an instant of total comprehension. Such moments most often arrive, we are told, in a site of natural beauty, as for example a garden, and may explain to some degree the Japanese obsession with gardens. Teachers of Zen, in attempting to awaken their students to the truth of Zen, expose them to ridicule and encourage them to spend weeks, months, even years, in the contemplation of riddles. Here is one such riddle: "A man is suspended over a cliff. He is holding on to the branch of a tree by his teeth, for his hands are tied. A friend looks down and asks him, 'What is Zen?' What should the man reply?" A moment of insight and understanding, transcending all rational and logical explanation, should eventually supply the answer—that there is no answer. Such truth is found not in the mind but in the heart, and only through silent meditation. Such is Zen.

What of Christianity in Japan? The Japanese people seem content with their non-Christian status. They do not persecute Christians, but neither do they join them. An American observer of the Japanese religious scene commented, "I wouldn't want to be a missionary in Japan, when after all these years only about half of one per cent are Christian. One missionary I know says he can honestly claim but five converts in five years."

Yet Christians have made a real contribution in Japan, in spite of the difficulties of proselytizing. They have built some of the finest schools and hospitals in the country and in so doing have aided the modernization of the people. Christianity's roots inJapan may be few, but they are deep. Still, the great majority of the Japanese show little or no interest in the works and prayers of Christians.

Nowadays, it is said that if the Japanese people do have a religion, it is for things. A Japanese friend put it this way: "Father is eager to buy a new electronic computer for his firm, Mother hankers after a new dishwasher, refrigerator or other electrical apparatus, while Son wonders how he can better his reputation or pass an examination. This wish for betterment may not strictly be a religion, but it leaves little time for anything else."

Yet, if this be true of the people of Japan today, if such is really their nature, one wonders why they crowd to the summer Bon Festival, for example, when the spirits of the dead are supposed to return to their native places. Is it through fear or superstition, or is it merely the desire to have a good time? Or why do they flock in such numbers to the new Buddhist sects such as Rissho Koseikai, with its Great Sacred Hall in Tokyo, or Soka Gakkai, with its temple in Shizuoka to which three million people make an annual pilgrimage? These two sects together claim fifteen million followers, while a dozen other new ones, eight of them with faith-healing doctrines, claim several million more. Yet it is true that these all appear to be more fraternal than religious. Their main concern is social welfare in the here and now. Both Rissho Koseikai and Soka Gakkai, for example, have schools, hospitals, homes for the aged, orchestras, group therapy, free movies, and very often free food. Soka Gakkai is in politics, too, a fact to which I shall give closer attention elsewhere.

But religion, whatever else it is in Japan, is a composite of feeling, ethic and philosophy, including extremes of melancholy and joy. These are extremes natural to the Japanese people, a sensitive people at once fearful and hopeful and easily offended by criticism.

"First thing they'll ask you," a visitor to Japan said to me on his return, "is, 'How do you like Japan?' They really want to know, too. That is, so long as you like Japan! They criticize themselves from time to time, but they only half mean it, or they are only trying to draw out a contradiction from you. They're absolutely loyal to the Land of the Rising Sun."

To which I rejoined, "They're not so very different from the rest of us, you mean."

Yet of course they are subject to some criticism, as are peoples everywhere. The truth is that Japan has a segregation problem even as we have, but it is not as well advertised as ours. There are perhaps a million Eta in Japan, living in their own communities, following their own tabooed trades, feeling the resentment of the outcast and showing it. These are the people who in feudal days were so low on the social scale that they were not even counted in the census. Above them were the nobles, the samurai, farmers, artisans and merchants, in that order. Lowest of all were the Eta. They were, and are, the butchers and skinners of animals, the tanners of hides, the workers in leather. The Meiji Reformation of 1868 emancipated the outcasts theoretically, but barriers which separated them from the people above them were slow in coming down. Perhaps greater absorption of Eta into accepted society has taken place since World War II than during the entire period from the Meiji Reformation up to the war.

But the problem, a deeply buried one that even some Japanese themselves never know, still remains, particularly when family backgrounds are checked prior to marriage. The discovery of Eta ancestry could, probably would, put an end to marriage plans. I have seen Eta communities in central Honshu and farther west in the Kansai area. From the outside they appear no different from the lower middle class areas surrounding them, and far better than any city slum area. It is not poverty, then, but occupations, or the occupations of their ancestry, that provide the reason for the outcast condition of these people. Enlightened Japanese are eager to have the Eta absorbed completely, to do away with the stigma attached to these several classes of workers and their offspring, and to raise their standards of living. I believe much has already been done, thanks in large measure to a former Eta who is now a highly respected member of the Japanese Diet.

And the Koreans in Japan are in a deplorable situation, generally speaking. Many of them fled there during the last war, adding considerably to the numbers who had already come as students or immigrants during the decades of Japan's rule in Korea. The people of Korea are a proud and noble race, broken by foreign rule and wars. In Japan, however, they are treated as inferiors. Most of them are working as day laborers or ragpickers. Many are members of the gangster element in Japan. Not that they want to be or would be if conditions were different, but even Koreans born in Japan find it very difficult to break into Japanese society. The empty feeling that they are neither Korean nor Japanese haunts them and fosters nihilism and decadence. The Japanese, in general, do consider themselves superior to other Asian peoples and especially so to those with darker skins, although they themselves are darker than most Koreans.

It is a sad truth, too, that although there is prejudice in Japan against all the Japanese children fathered by American soldiers, the ones who suffer the most are those who are partly Negro. Undeniably, there is race prejudice in Japan, but it is not quite the same sort of prejudice as ours. Even the Koreans are discriminated against not so much for their color as for their lack of national identity. They have mixed with the Japanese people, yet they are not Japanese. It is much the same with children of foreign parentage. Black or white, the father is not Japanese, and therefore the child is not Japanese. He does not belong. This attitude is less an expression of prejudice against a group than an outgrowth of nationalism. The Japanese have kept themselves to themselves for so long that they cannot readily accept the introduction of a foreign strain. A group, white or black, belongs in its "proper place," and when it is in its proper place it is treated with respect. Non-Japanese or half-Japanese children are accepted readily into schools, and non-Japanese businessmen of all races are received without question. But intermarriage and less formal unions between Japanese and foreigner are not generally acceptable. The couple may be tolerated and even kindly treated, but the children of such unions always encounter prejudice. The child who is part Negro suffers additionally from what seems to be a world-wide preference for light-colored skins. I make no attempt to explain this preference; I can only say that it does exist. The Japanese certainly share it. Those whom they consider the most beautiful and handsome amongst themselves are those with the fairest skin.

There is another form of discrimination that is perhaps even more saddening. It has its roots in Hiroshima and Nagasaki, and concerns the people who were there at the time of the holocaust. The mental and psychological scars are countless and incalculable, but there are many people who bear their scars on their bodies for the world to see. One would hope that those who bear them would be the recipients of special consideration. But the cruel truth is that if these damaged people try to enter, let us say, a public swimming pool, all the other bathers get out. To their never-ending hurt, the scarred ones are cautiously avoided wherever they go, and even those who have no visible traces of wounds but who are known to have been exposed to radiation are shunned as if suspected of harboring the seeds of horrors to come. Thus the victims of twenty years ago are victims still.

Yet the dead are mourned. On the banks of the Ota River, which runs through Hiroshima, there is a scarred and twisted building now called the Atomic Dome. It has been left there, in its ruins, as a memorial to the past. Once a year, on August 6, the anniversary of that day of pain and death, paper lanterns bearing lighted candles float downstream past the skeletal dome. On August 9 of each year, too, lanterns with their flickering lights float, like dying souls, down Nagasaki's river into the bay and out to sea. Each one is dedicated to the departed spirit of an A-bomb victim. Both dates are solemnly observed, both occasions reminders of what must never happen again. Yet these ceremonies are not without relief, for on the special days of memory the spirits of the dead are said to visit those they loved in life.

XII

IN VIEW OF the apparent Japanese agnosticism, if that is indeed what it is, it is almost strange that there are so very many occasions with religious overtones. But, whether the Japanese people are religious or not, whether their shrines are sacred to a cult or meccas for holiday crowds, whether the pilgrimages and spectacles are spiritual, fraternal, or due to love of festival for its own sake, it is a fact that there is some sort of festival or celebration throughout the country on practically every day of the year.

All Japan celebrates a reunion with the dead during the annual Bon Festival, a Buddhist festival often called the Feast of Lanterns because lantern light plays so great a part in it. The Bon Festival takes place for three days during summer.

While such a festival for the dead may be thought to be a solemn occasion, it is also a time of joy and festivity, for the souls of all dead loved ones return briefly for a reunion with the living. Houses are carefully cleaned for the occasion and special foods are prepared for the honored visitors, unseen and incorporeal though they may be. On the first two days of celebration the people visit graveyards and burn incense to the departed, not to remote ancestors, for that is not Japanese custom, but to those of recent generations who are remembered by some who are left. After their devotions, the people invite their spirit relatives to their homes, where food is waiting in small special bowls. As darkness falls, lanterns are lit in cemeteries and outside homes, and glowworms of light glimmer in the night.

On the last day of festival, bands play, and there is dancing and singing of Bon Odori songs. All, or almost all, is gaiety and laughter, for this is not meant to be a sad occasion. With the close of day, bonfires are lit in farewell to the temporary guests, and the lanterns, each representing a soul, are cast into a river and floated out into the unknown sea. Still there is happiness and revelry, and still there are smiles, but some of the smiles hide fresh grief. And some faces do not hide their sorrow. A face watching a lantern bob upon the water may be wet with tears. For it is not true that the Japanese people always hide their emotions, nor that they are expected to. These are human feelings, to be expressed at the proper time and in the proper place, although on certain occasions they must be concealed for fear of spreading sorrow to others. Consideration enters here and also, of course, custom. It is not thought right to mourn openly for a departed child, for the death of a little one is Fate and to grieve is to rebel against the gods. But the death of an older person, a revered parent for instance, is a proper occasion on which to show grief. The death of a husband, too, is expected to call forth tears, and it would be considered very odd if a bereaved wife did not cry, and cry aloud, in public. Thus the gaiety of the Bon Festival is always touched with sadness, especially for those whose loss has not been eased by time, and longing thoughts go with the lanterns as they drift, small beacons to guide the spirits on their way, through the night toward the sea. One of the Bon Odori songs reflects this inner sadness:

Now the Bon has come,
A man without passion
Is like a wooden or a metal Buddha,
Or one of stone.

And the Japanese are not made of stone.

Often the Japanese enthusiasm for festival is combined with their love of beauty. During the cherry blossom season and, indeed, at many other times of the year, pilgrims flock to the unique and lovely island of Miyajima. There, in the midst of loveliness, they celebrate the annual Shrine Festival, the Festival Bidding the Old Year Out, the Longevity Festival, and whatever else they feel like celebrating. I have spent many happy hours on Miyajima, and hope to do so again. It is a small island, only nineteen miles in circumference, but exquisite as a gem in the setting of the Inland Sea. The great shrine of Itsukushima, with its lofty camphorwood torii, is built on the edge of the sea, so close indeed that when the tide rises it seems to float upon the waves. So revered is the shrine that the whole island is considered sacred. No one is permitted to make his home there, no birth can take place, no burial is allowed. It is forbidden even to cut trees, and deer roam in a virgin forest that is one of the few left in Japan.

Miyajima is always beautiful, from seashore to the peak of Mount Misen, but most so, perhaps, at cherry blossom season. Then, alas, it is also too crowded. Yet one can accept the crowd, for not only the blossoms but the ceremonial dance, the powerful *bugaku,* can now be seen. It is an elaborately costumed, ritualistic ceremony that is performed by only one family, and this has been true for the past eight centuries. At special times the Shinto priests perform their own religious dance, the *kagura,* and this on the most beautiful and ancient dance floor in the world, I daresay. It is made of very wide boards of camphorwood and is the original floor of the more than thousand-year-old shrine.

Here there is also the Senjo-kaku, Hideyoshi's Hall of a Thousand Mats, even if they are less than half that number, with the thousands of good luck rice scoops that surround its inner shrine. The rice scoops are prayer messages hung up within the big hall before and around the inner shrine. Each is inscribed with the name of the giver and a prayer or good luck message for a family member or beloved friend.

Far away, to the north, a very different kind of spectacle may be observed, though seldom by tourists or casual visitors. This is the Ainu Bear Festival on Hokkaido. The Ainu, as I have said, worship sun, wind and stars as well as many other natural phenomena, and the bear, their favorite "god." The part of the festival that is least likely to be seen is the capture of the bear. Ainu hunters search for them in caves and having located their quarry, plant several poles in front of the cave and wait for what they know will develop. The bear, it seems, is attracted by the entertainment possibilities of the poles, and emerges playfully to dig them up. The hunters draw their bowstrings while he is thus engaged, if their intent is to skin him, and send their arrows flying. If the bear is young and tender they will spare him temporarily and save him for the festival called *Iyomande,* feeding him with loving care and special food until the big day dawns. Then, plump as he is, he is ceremoniously executed by arrow, and eaten as the main course of a three-day feast. To the Ainu there is nothing cruel in all this. The body of the bear, they will tell you, is nothing but a prison for a trapped spirit who is eager to be released. Since only the flesh is eaten the spirit is of course free to return to its heavenly home, there to bask in a glow of gratitude toward his Ainu rescuers and lend his good offices in their times of need.

Throughout Japan there are shrines and temples too numerous to mention, much less to describe, but they are such a part of Japanese life that I must touch upon a few. In addition to the famous Grand Shrine of Ise, and the shrine city of Kyoto, there are the less well known shrines and temples of Nara, which include the seventh-century Gango-ji temple, and the Shosoin or Treasure House, the oldest storehouse in the world, built in the year 756 A.D., which contains the priceless objects gathered for use in the extravagant ceremonies held in celebration of the completion of the Great Buddha. The Treasure House is sealed up fifty weeks out of the year and opened only during the crisp, dry days of the last week in October and the first week in November so that the priceless objects within may be aired and examined. It is a privileged visitor who sees it during that brief period, for a visit to the Treasure House is a trip through time.

In Inuyama are two shrines which are, I would say, two of the most amazing attractions in all Japan, perhaps in all Asia. They are two shrines dedicated to the reproductive organs, male and female. To the shrines of Inuyama the Japanese often come to get married, and after the ceremony they pose for their formal wedding pictures beside the phallic symbols of their choice. During shrine festivals, these amazingly realistic objects, several as big as telephone poles, are paraded through the streets. How the amulets sold at these shrines ever get through customs I will never know, but I assume that a good many do for they are among the most cherished items brought back into this country by visitors to Japan.

And near to Inuyama in the Gifu hinterland are such places as Shirakawa, where the old five-story ladder farmhouses still function, with their thirty to fifty inhabitants, and where life has not changed in any but superficial ways for a hundred years. Gifu itself is a city of 200,000, but somehow I always think of it as a town. This is the place where those old wooden Toonerville trolley cars from bygone San Francisco days still operate between the main part of town and the river, where they hold the cormorant fishing spectacle from May to October. It is true that the spectacle, which takes place on the Nagara River just at dusk, has little to do with fish, although cormorant fishing is still widely practiced in Japan. Rather, it is a dance of boats upon a river stage with a backdrop of mountain and castle, and it goes back a thousand years into antiquity.

Along the river's edge, or being poled upstream against the current, are hundreds of low, red-roofed *yakata* boats, their blue lanterns lit and swaying. From them come the sounds of singing and laughter and the plaintive strains of the samisen. Along the shore, yukata-clad hotel guests watch the movement of the boats, the occasional fireworks, and particularly the beautiful float of dancing geishas that moves up and down the river, its music almost lost at times and then heard again as the float comes back downstream. From the far shore the hills of Gifu rise steep, atop them Mount Kinka castle, outlined with lanterns against the sky.

Eventually the bow flare of the leading cormorant boat appears upstream, and like dancers on a giant stage the pleasure boats make way for the star, the leading boat. More cormorant boats follow the leader, and with torches flaring at the bow and handlers juggling their birds to keep them clear and the lines free, the fishing boats swiftly move downstream. At the widest part of the river they hold fast in a horizontal line as pleasure craft move onstage for the grand finale. Because I think of it as a spectacle, I prefer to watch cormorant fishing from the shore. But I have heard it said that most people, men at any rate, would rather ride with their geisha in a yakata boat and get a closer look. At the cormorants, of course!

In Tokyo are found two of the largest and most frequented temples in Japan. One is the Zojoji, which still has its original two-story red gate, the oldest and largest temple gate in the city. Within its precincts are four magnificent mausoleums of Tokugawa shoguns, the oldest dating back to 1635. The Japanese people, religious or not, visit the Zojoji in their hundreds and thousands.

The other, the Asakusa Kannon Temple, might be called a "working" temple, for it is always crowded with visitors who throng there day and night to offer their prayers. I have particularly enjoyed my visits there because, unlike the great temples of Kyoto and Nara, it is not on the itinerary of sightseeing buses with their loads of tourists. Those who visit go there for quiet thought, for meditation. Just to sit on a bench nearby gives one a feeling for the country and the people. On the one side, at the monastery, one can see the Japanese genius for creating peace and tranquility in the throbbing heart of the city. On the other, a mere stone's throw away, is graphic proof of the need for such an oasis of quiet beauty in the midst of ugliness, for here is the old Yoshiwara district, the old red light section of Tokyo. It is not what it used to be since the 1958 prostitution law, but it is still hardly a cultural center. This is another of the Japanese paradoxes: peace and beauty hidden amidst uproar and ugliness. Indeed, it is Japanese nature to pursue peaceful contemplation with the same fervor that they pursue the pleasures of the pool hall, to devote their attention equally to kabuki plays, nō drama, strip-tease exhibitions and poor films, to appreciate baseball as well as *bonsai,* to enjoy the quietude of their gardens as well as the roar of the race track.

XIII

It is Japanese nature, too, to seek pleasure wherever it can be found. I dare say that, per square mile and per capita, Japan has more places of amusement than any country in the world. I know the places of amusement that a rich and varied nature bestows on them, but I do not count seashore, mountains, flowers, forests or hot springs. I think now of museums, art galleries, theaters, motion pictures, bars; baseball fields, sports fields indeed of every kind; feasts, festivals, sake parties, prize fighting, judo, skating rinks that stay open night and day in order to satisfy the endless crowds of skaters; ski spots where skiers line up hours in advance for the lifts; the thousand-acre play complex of Yomiuriland, outside Tokyo, where a huge snowless ski jump operates the year round, where there are two golf courses, one private, fabulously expensive and oversubscribed the year before it opened, a chain of fish ponds, heavily stocked, a clubhouse with a geodesic dome, and a monorail to take visitors from one play place to another.

Yes, the Japanese today are a people who enjoy life almost with frenzy. Picnics and tours to famous places are part of education for school children, and any beauty spot or ancient monument is crowded with well-behaved children in uniforms, each with his or her knapsack and lunch box. I well remember an overnight sea trip to the volcanic island of Oshima, off the eastern coast near Tokyo. The steamship was crowded with school children and their teachers, a top-heavy old ship that rolled all night to dangerous angles. The children suffered piteously from seasickness but appeared bravely ready, in the early morning, to undertake the long climb up the black lava flanks of Oshima's volcano. Both teachers and children were determined to enjoy themselves, suffer though they might in the attempt.

Night life, at least in Tokyo, is quieter than it was. A new law was passed in August 1964 requiring bars and cabarets to close at midnight. They do, for the most part, although of course some of them wear a new face and make a show of serving food in a six-to-four ratio to liquor in order to stay open past the curfew. Otherwise, the busiest and most popular places are the *sushi* bars, and since sushi is nothing more than the equivalent of a sandwich, or fishy snack, the sushi bar can hardly be described as a den of iniquity. Night life for the average Tokyo resident is not, therefore, nearly as exciting as rumor would have it.

But there is gambling. The Japanese love to gamble, whether it be at the bicycle or horse racing track, or at their version of the one-armed bandit so popular in Nevada. The game of pachinko has been described by some observers as the Great National Pastime, and I think quite accurately.

No report on Japan would be complete without a description of pachinko, the favored sport of Todai students. It is a pinball game that has grown to outlandish proportions in Japanese cities. Take the city of Nagoya, for instance. In Nagoya there are approximately 30,000 machines in 196 pachinko parlors, which are the most garish buildings with the most brilliant neon lights in town. Some are several stories high, with hundreds of vertical pachinko machines, row on row, in almost constant use from ten in the morning to ten at night. Music blaring from a loudspeaker is scarcely audible over the din of the pachinko balls. I am not an expert, but I know that it is played something like this:

For a hundred yen (twenty-eight cents when I was last there) a player receives fifty small metal balls. These he endeavors to shoot into any one of eight cups on the pachinko board. For each success the machine automatically feeds back fifteen balls to the player. Speed of play is rapid, and the fifty balls could be used up in a minute if none paid off. But rarely is this the case, particularly for the experienced player. There is some skill involved, usually in picking the right machine, and police estimate that in Nagoya alone there are from five hundred to a thousand pachinko *professionals* who play all day long and eke out a living in the process. There are no cash prizes; the winners turn in their winnings for groceries, cigarettes, or some particular household item which can be taken around the corner and exchanged for cash. This is not legal, but it is done.

Most people who enter the pachinko parlors, however, are not professionals but casual players, stopping by in the lunch hour, on the way to classes, on the way to work, or between shopping trips to department stores. Their ventures are not always losing propositions. But, of course, the machines win eventually, and only the owners get rich. Pachinko, in fact, is the main source of revenue for the highly organized *yakuza,* the gangster element in Japan. The eventual losers must always be the players, even though they make occasional gains, and sad to say, students and young businessmen have been known to commit suicide after squandering all their resources at the pachinko boards. Such is pachinko's hypnotic allure that at any given moment between the hours of four and ten P.M. there are perhaps a million people throughout Japan, in varying degrees of pachinko hypnosis, feeding in their money and playing the game. It is a sad waste of time and money, even of life. Perhaps it is also a reflection of a not uncommon Japanese feeling that life, after all, is quite meaningless. I am not sure that this is so, but it may be.

There are, of course, other sports. Most Japanese would prefer to proclaim sumo, not pachinko, the chief sport of the nation. Certainly it is older, for it dates back to Caesar's time. The participants are immense men, often more than three hundred and sometimes over four hundred pounds in weight, who, after a great deal of ritual, attempt to throw each other down on the sand-covered wrestling mat or out of the fifteen-foot ring. Preliminary ceremony is long, matches are short. It is the pageantry of sumo, rather than its excitement as a sport, that keeps it popular. Here is how it goes. Two enormous men, clad only in minuscule loin cloths, each fringed with a tiny apron, enter the sandbag-encircled room and greet each other with elaborate salutations. A referee in ancient, traditional costume introduces them to the audience in equally ancient traditional phrases and almost inaudible voice, and then they leave the inner circle and go to their respective sides of the ring. Here, by the corner posts that support the canopy over the ring, are tubs or buckets of water. Each waddling giant now washes his hands, rinses out his mouth, and sprinkles a pinch of salt into the ring. All this is a purification rite. When it is over, or apparently over, the men crouch low in the ring and face each other unblinkingly with their great hamlike hands before them on the mat. Each waits, with elephantine caution, for an opening, for the one right moment to attack. According to sumo rules, however, there is no chance for sneak attack or sudden lunge, for the contestants are supposed to rise at the same instant. If they do not they must go through the preliminaries all over again. After perhaps five minutes of false start and repurifying they lumber into action. The bout may last as long as a few minutes, but it is usually over in thirty seconds. It may end with one behemoth forcing some part of the other's body, apart from his feet, down onto the mat, or it may end more spectacularly with one of them flipping the other out of the ring, an amazing sight.

The bout over, two more vast figures enter the ring, this time clad in beautiful and costly embroidered aprons. These are champions, not scheduled for the wrestling events of the evening, but who are appearing instead as performers of the ring entry ceremony. They clap their hands, stamp their feet, and retire to ringside after some time to watch the next bout. During sumo tournaments there may be dozens of matches each day over a period of fifteen days, all of which are watched avidly by ringside crowds, who bring their lunch and take off their shoes, and millions of television viewers. Sumo champions are admired and almost revered by Japanese fans, who idolize their mountainous wrestlers as if they were national heroes.

If it were not for ancient sumo, modern baseball would be *the* national sport. The Japanese have baseball clubs and leagues just as we do, their Pacific and Central Leagues corresponding to our American and National Leagues, and an enthusiasm for the sport and its stars that sometimes even exceeds our own. There is some difference in the style of play. Japanese baseball puts more stress on the bunt, the squeeze, the double play and the one-run inning, and it is not the power game it is in the States. As a matter of fact, baseball is a fairly recent addition to the Japanese sports scene, having become popular only since the time Lefty O'Doul, Babe

Ruth, Joe DiMaggio and other big leaguers went to Japan for exhibition games in the twenties and thirties.

The Japanese play a great deal of tennis, too, but with a flat-topped racket and a ball softer than ours in the West. The stroke is from the wrist and forearm rather than from the shoulder, and overspin is the key. Again, it is not a power game, but rather one of subtlety. And then of course there is American-style pro wrestling, as distinct from sumo, and there is very little subtlety or skill in this. Some histrionic ability is required, for it is entertainment and not sport in the true sense, just as it is in the United States. The extent to which it has caught on in a Japan that fully appreciates judo, kendo, sumo and karate is amazing.

When the Japanese play anything, they play hard, even if not with powerful style. Japanese men and women enjoy their sports with desperate seriousness. They feel it a moral obligation, a duty to the nation, to excel, especially in international sports; and to compensate for their relatively shorter height and lighter weight, they develop toughness and endurance. Indeed, their national pride is so strong that they will take up a sport they do not particularly care for and train themselves until they are exceptionally good at it. For instance, they do not on the whole care very much for swimming, and yet they have so trained themselves that they are frequent winners in international swimming meets. Swimming, of course, requires the very qualities that they are best able to develop, and since they do have the capacity to be good at it they feel they must excel whether they enjoy it or not.

It is also true that the Japanese do not have the "sporting" sense on which we pride ourselves. It is not part of their tradition. Everybody dislikes losing, but Japanese hate it and do not hesitate to show their feelings. It is not unusual for a Japanese athlete, or even a whole team, to indulge in a great public display of disappointment after losing. Onlookers are astonished by their weeping and gnashing of teeth, especially those who have grown up believing in the myth that the Japanese either do not have emotions or never show them, or with the conviction that one must be a sporting loser. The Japanese look at it quite differently. They feel very deeply about many things, and losing is one of them. To them, this is a perfectly proper occasion on which to show emotion. If they lose, they will not pretend that they are not sorry; they wish they had won, and they show it. If they want to cry, they cry. It is all quite logical, and human.

The logic of it can be carried one step further, and sometimes is. I remember one occasion when I was visiting a Japanese university. They had a brand-new football team which they had carefully trained for its first match, to be played against a rival college. They sent the team off with great fanfare and waited eagerly for their return. When they came back next day they asked them, "Who won?"

They said, "We didn't play."

"You didn't?"

"No, there was no sense in playing, because the other team was better than ours!"

XIV

YET NOT ALL is frenzy in the Japanese enjoyment of life. Their pursuit of the more obvious pleasures is matched by their genuine delight in the beauties of Nature and the rewards of meditation in solitude. On the one hand they are gay and outgoing, and on the other they are contemplative and introspective. With their deep love for everything beautiful they make art objects of the most simple articles of daily life and enjoyable rituals of the most ordinary actions. The taking of a bath, for instance, is not considered a necessity, but a marvelous opportunity for relaxation. Eating utensils are colorful and attractive to the eye. Food is presented in such a manner that the mere sight of it is delectable, and the eye feasts before the body.

Eating in Japan is a pleasure, a pastime, an artistic delight, and must be so considered at least by the visitor unaccustomed to the combination. Let us begin with breakfast. If one is staying in a room at an old-fashioned Japanese inn, the quilts and mattresses are first put away neatly into wall closets, bedrooms become living rooms, and a cheerful maid moves the low table into the middle of the room, sets the seat cushion before it, and then brings in breakfast.

In one of three small bowls is a raw egg. In the second is rice. In the third is a soup made of bean paste and containing, perhaps, Japanese leek, clams, fried bean curd, spinach or something like it. One beats the egg with chopsticks, adds *shoyu* (soy) sauce, then pours the egg with shoyu over the rice. With the rice-and-egg mixture and the soup, one eats pickled vegetables—pickled eggplant, or ginger or cucumber, for example. Other things might be in the soup, of course. Thin sheets of dried seaweed are a common addition. But by and large, that is breakfast and it is good. Many Japanese families now eat an American breakfast. I don't know why, for to me their breakfast is delicious, but they have come to like oatmeal and porridge and fried eggs.

Lunch may be a bowl of noodles with vegetables and a little pork, served in a very tasty fish stock. This is the typical inn lunch, and though I have always enjoyed it I know that it may seem insubstantial to some. I remember, by way of contrast, a little restaurant in Nagoya that used to serve, and perhaps still serves, a much more substantial but still quite simple meal. It was a clean, cool place with a fountain in the center, and many pretty waitresses who served the six-course luncheon of the day on lacquered trays, with hot Japanese tea, all for a hundred yen, or twenty-eight cents. The six courses were salad, soup, rice, tempura, vegetables, and fish or meat, small portions but tasty and quite sufficient. In this restaurant, as in all Japanese restaurants, there was no tipping. There is very little tipping anywhere in Japan; it is not considered nice. In fact, Japan is the only country in the world, that I know of, where tips are refused. I have known cases of taxi drivers who, after inadvertently accepting extra money, have run after their passengers to give their money back. In the few cases where tips are acceptable, such as to one's private maid at the old-fashioned Japanese inn, the offering must be wrapped and given quietly, without flourish. I mention this because I think it casts light on the Japanese character. They do not like the business of handling money, and they do not like accepting gratuities for hospitable services.

On a recent visit to Japan I went with some Japanese friends to the town of Kozoji in central Honshu, and stopped for dinner at an inn overlooking the Tamano River. I was their first non-Japanese guest in over a year. The private dining room had the usual tatami and low table, and *zabuton* on which to sit, or squat, whichever you prefer. The three of us were served by four kimono-clad waitresses who sat with us during the meal and took part in the conversation. The food was excellent.

To start with came the traditional bean paste cakes and Japanese green tea. Then fish eggs over crushed *daikon,* which is comparable to our radish. *Sashimi* next, choice pieces of raw bream, delicate little fragments decorated with cherry blossoms. Then, bits of raw squid, cut in small squares and covered with melted cheese, *tofu* wrapped in tender seaweed, and a cooked vegetable called *warabi* that tastes something like a combination of celery and asparagus. All these foods were eaten with the small Japanese chopsticks after first being dipped into an appetizing soy sauce.

After this came *sashimi suimono,* a clear soup with raw fish in it, and boiled bamboo shoots with boiled fish, chicken with *miso* paste and raw vegetables, boiled shrimp dipped in a mild vinegar sauce, rice covered with shredded egg and *nori,* a bean soup called *akadashi,* and of course *tsukemono,* the pickled vegetables served with any meal. Finally, strawberries and sliced banana, dipped in powdered sugar. I must say I could not manage all of this, but it was a most delectable meal.

Many Westerners dislike the idea of raw fish, and the great quantities of rice in the Japanese diet. But the fish is ocean fresh, cut into tiny little pieces and seasoned delicately, pleasing to the most fastidious palate and the most jaded appetite. And the rice, too, is wonderfully cooked, delicately flavored, beautiful to look at and feather light. I have lived for weeks and months at a time on Japanese food and I have always liked it. It is light and healthy, in a way like Chinese food but not so rich and perhaps not so varied, though it has something for all tastes. One easily loses weight on it for there are no rich sauces or anything difficult to digest. I find Japanese food really wonderful, and I enjoyed every week at my Japanese inn and every visit to a restaurant.

The Japanese seldom entertain in their homes, for they think that their humble abode is not good enough for a guest, but when they do, they offer their guests a bath, much as we would offer cocktails. More often than not they reserve this courtesy for their Japanese friends, but I myself have had this experience. I must say they always defer to my being a Westerner, and I have not been asked to bathe with the family. The courteous Japanese host will usually ask his guest to use the bath first. When the guest has finished, the family will follow in order of seniority. Father, of course, is always senior to Mother, age regardless.

A Westerner's first visit to a Japanese home is full of surprises. First there is the bath habit, and then there is the question of privacy. The Japanese have their own standards of privacy, and they are not quite the same as ours. Early in the morning a little maid comes into the guest's room, with a smile but without knocking, to offer the same services she offers to the rest of the household. She makes up your bed, helps

OPPOSITE
Ainu girls. Hokkaido.

21-11
KAN

Mother and baby at bus stop. Northern Honshu.

Contrasts are everywhere; the modern and traditional walk side by side. In country and city alike, people follow the old ways simultaneously with the new.

Family breakfast. Northern Honshu.

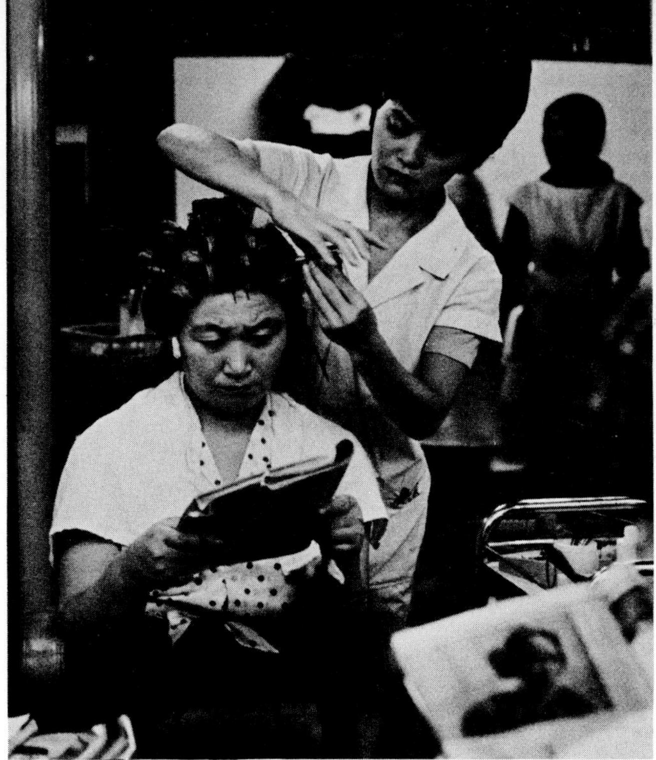

Beauty salon. Tokyo.

Shinto wedding. Tokyo.

Public bath. Tokyo.

Actresses during rehearsal break. Tokyo.

They are as up-to-date as the rest of the world...

Laboratory technician. Nippon Oil Company.

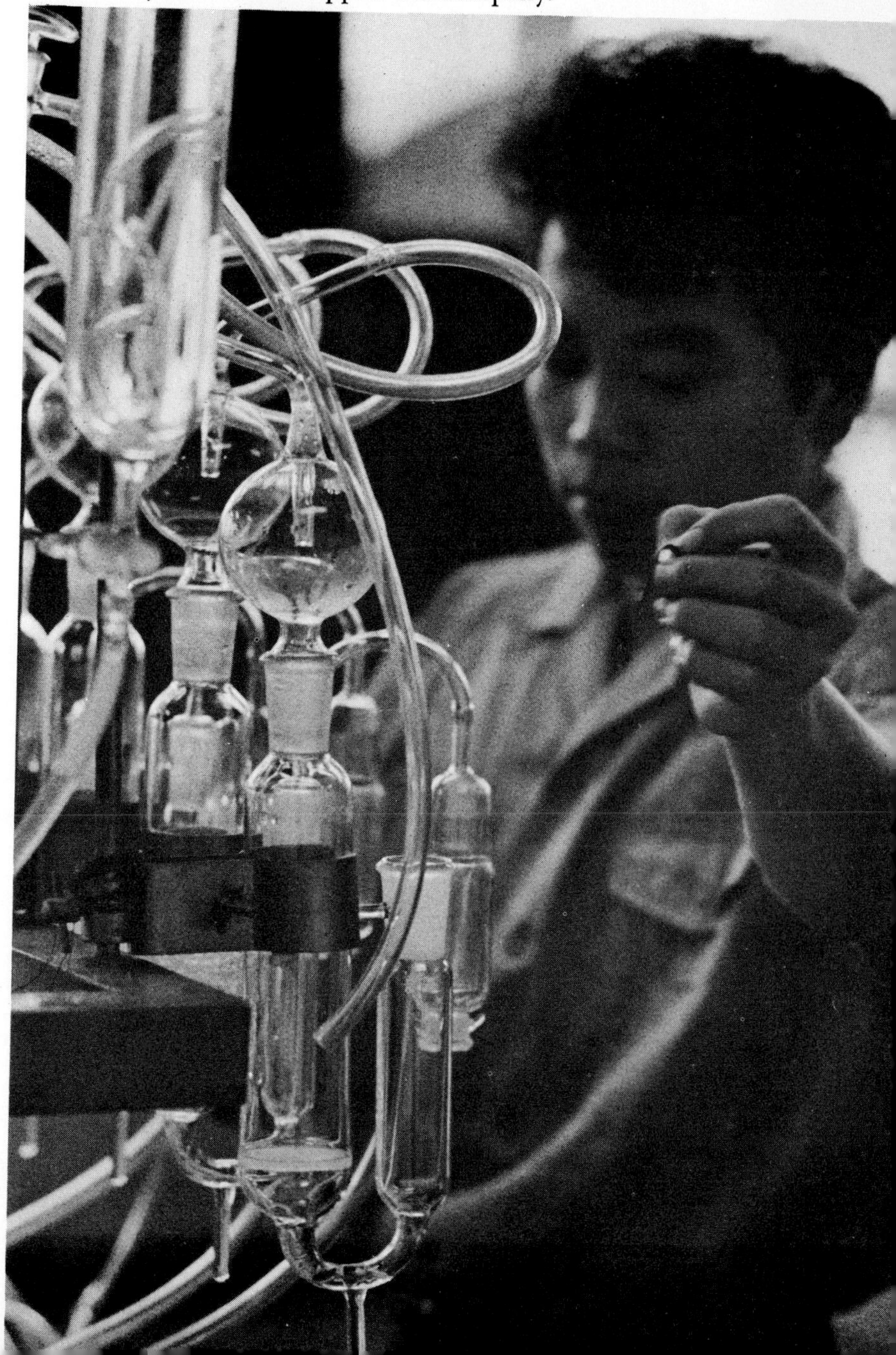

Newspaper office. Tokyo.

Department store dummy. Kyoto.

Sound-recording engineer. Tokyo.

At the Coca-Cola plant.

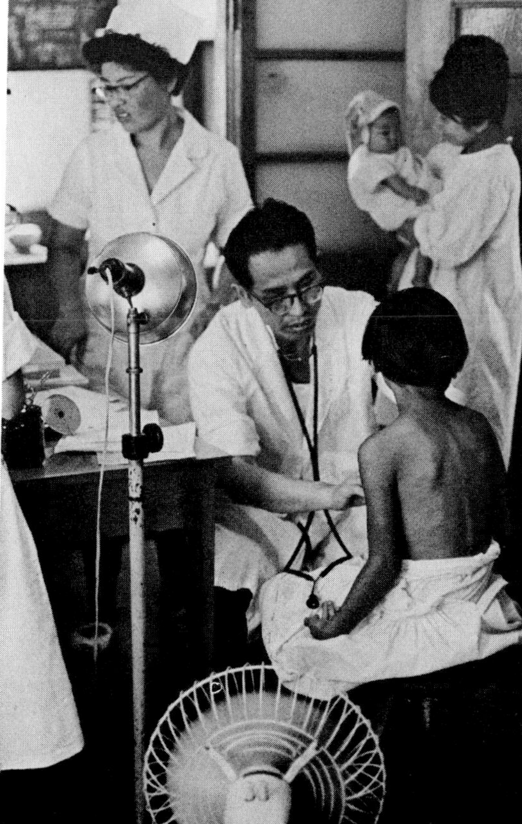

Country doctor at work.
North of Nagasaki, Kyushu.

Family excursion. Honshu.

...and they move as swiftly.

Yet now, above all, they desire peace.

Schoolchildren at the Peace Memorial. Hiroshima.

They retain their strong love of learning, though it now turns upon new forms...

Music teacher conducting *Finlandia*. Tokyo.

At the blackboard. Aomori, Honshu.

Ballet students. Kyoto.

Schoolboys. Tokyo.

Ivy League University. Tokyo.

Morning at the orphanage.
Aomori, Honshu.

...and their reverence for the ancient customs remains firmly rooted.

Tea ceremony.

The Great Buddha of Beppu. Kyushu.

Shinto Shrine. Tokyo.

Shinto Shrine. Northern Honshu.

Meditation. Daisen-in, Kyoto.

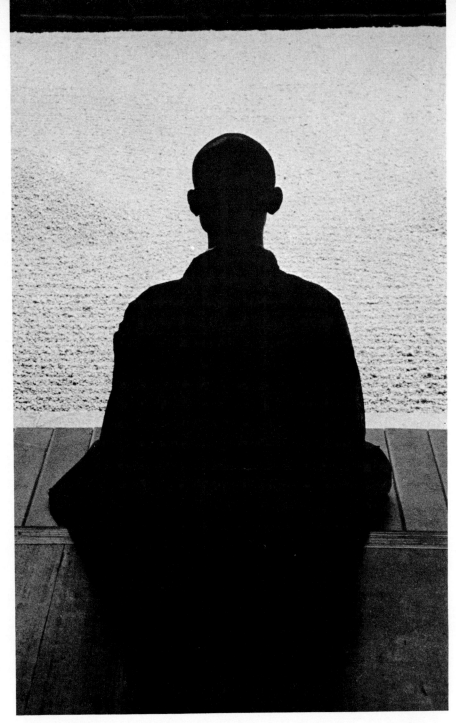

Underlying all of the changes in the people of Japan, the unchanging, timeless values continue to prevail.

you with your clothes and your bath, and then leaves you briefly to get your breakfast. Then, usually, she will sit with you while you eat. This is disconcerting to Westerners, for the little maids come and go without a by-your-leave and perform services that you have not had since you were a child. That you may be stark naked and doing your morning exercises when she enters does not concern her in the least. She simply goes about her business with her happy smile and cheery chatter. I only know by hearsay how a man must feel about it, and for myself I have been used to it all my life, but I do remember a guest in China who was once very surprised. Once only, for the next time she was prepared.

In the China of those days all the servants were male. I do not know how it is today, although I suppose there are no longer any house servants, but then Chinese families had their houseboys, valued members of the household. My guests on this occasion were very *English* English, and I had carefully instructed my houseboy always to knock before he entered their room. He forgot these instructions one day and walked straight in on the lady. Seeing the condition that she was in—undressed, I can only presume, for no one gave details—he turned around immediately and with great politeness, walked out, shut the door, and *then* knocked.

This sort of thing happens quite often in Japan, except that it happens to men, because in Japan the servants are always women. My men friends tell me that the maids walk into their rooms, just as they always have into mine, and offer to scrub their backs in the tub and perform all manner of polite courtesies to which the American male is not accustomed. The maids think nothing of the nakedness of their guests, or of whatever condition they may be in, but the men are often quite embarrassed at first. Then of course they get used to being pampered, and begin to wonder why they do not receive the same treatment from their wives.

No, customs and ways of thinking are not always easy to get used to. We seem to be very different, we Americans and our Japanese friends. Yet we are not. The more we know about each other, the less our differences will seem, and more complete understanding will come eventually if we continue to make meaningful contact with each other. We have become accustomed to British understatement and Irish hyperbole; why should we not, now, accept and understand Japanese ambiguity? When we do, we will see that our differences are more apparent than real, and that some of the barriers between us are not barriers but merely fences.

It is hard to know how to give and receive the gift of love, even hard sometimes to recognize it for what it is. Contrary to Western belief, the Japanese are a warm and demonstrative people. If you have reached them and they feel your warmth for them, they will respond with an even greater warmth that has nothing to do with form, politeness, tradition. They do not kiss, for that is not their custom, but they come to you with open arms and put those arms around you. They hold your hand; they give you small, carefully selected and beautifully wrapped gifts, and they serve you in every way they know. Your happiness is their concern, so they try to take you to beautiful places and show you things they think will make you happy, and then they will hold your hand again.

It has been said, too, that the Japanese, because of their rigid and sometimes artificial code of discipline, have little sense of humor. I myself think that this is disproved in many of their writings, if nothing else, but it is quite true that they are not sure of laughter. I think they have become a little confused by humor, or rather the means of expressing their appreciation of it, because in the past they were taught to laugh artificially to hide their feelings rather than to show them. Having used laughter as a means of concealing pain and embarrassment, they find it difficult to laugh spontaneously at what we think of as the right times. Yet, without having a finely honed wit, they do appreciate humor, they do have a sense of the ridiculous, and they do sometimes laugh as readily as any American.

When I lived in the little village in Kyushu, there was a motion picture theater right across the way and I went to see many Japanese films. The audiences consisted mostly of men, because someone had to take care of the children and it would not occur to a man to do that, so there they were without their wives and enjoying themselves hugely. If one wishes to see really bad movies, one can see them in Japan, for the producers turn them out by the thousands and there is no time for quality. With few exceptions the plot is sex and violence, sex and violence, and at least one rape scene.

I remember one evening the girl in the film got raped by almost everybody, and the cast was not small. The first time it happened the men in the audience sat with their eyes glued to the screen. By the third time they began to get a little bored. At the fifth raping they burst into roars of laughter, and after that every rape scene was greeted with a loud guffaw. There are many such examples, some showing a touch of cruelty, some showing a great deal of subtlety, but all suggesting that the Japanese have a great deal of humor.

It is also commonly believed that the Japanese have what I might call a strong herd instinct and that they are afraid to be different from their fellows. This, to a large extent, is true. There is a strong strain of individualism in them, particularly among their writers and artists, but on the whole they tend very much to do what others do. They have conformed for centuries, and they are conforming now. This is particularly true when they are thinking in terms of family and parents, but it is true in other areas as well. Even in their dress they do not like to show individuality. The young man who leaves college and puts on the gray flannel suit of the zaibatsu is one example, and there are many such. For all Japanese there is a proper attire for everything and a proper time to change. With the official arrival of summer the coats come off and the sea of white shirts on the station platforms is overwhelming. Not green, gray, blue, red, yellow, brown, tan, or even off-white. No, white to the right, white to the left, so ride the six million on their way to work.

This conformism permeates Japanese life, and customs and formalities still hold firm, especially in the upper and middle strata. For instance, a young American friend of mine wanted to take his Japanese wife to the beach on the fifteenth of June. It was a hot day, he told me, and perfect for swimming. But his wife objected strenuously because, as she said, "It's not the first of July yet!" Japan being a man's country, they went anyway. The young wife was very embarrassed at being party to such a social error, but she need not have been. No one saw them, for there was not another soul in sight. On July 1, the official beginning of summer and therefore the right time to go to the beach, they went again. The day was foggy and unpleasant, but the beach was crowded.

Summer is also the time to climb Mount Fuji. Climbing season begins, with the swimming, on July 1, so up they go for 12,000 feet, four and five abreast like shoppers at a bargain sale. Why? Because it is the thing to do. Of course this is not the only day on which the Japanese climb Fuji, for they love their mountain and visit it frequently on summer weekends, but it is the day most favored by custom. Spring greenery and autumnal tints hold few attractions for the hiker. Summer is the only really right time to climb.

The autumnal full moon is said by the Japanese to be the year's most beautiful. Whether because of this moon or because of the turning leaves, Japanese women always go around wearing expressions of tender melancholy in the autumn. It is the traditional time for sweet sadness and poetic thoughts.

These are not, of course, alarming examples of Japanese collective-mindedness, but they do reveal something of the strong Japanese tendency to function as part of a group rather than as individuals.

Does this conformism mean that the Japanese would make good followers for some demagogue yet to emerge? Yes, there is always the danger, because such men have emerged in the past, although it is true that they were iconoclastic demagogues rather than nationalists. The danger lies not so much, perhaps, with a demagogue as with a demagogic faction, for the Japanese are more inclined to follow movements than individuals. Take for example the rise of the Soka Gakkai. It grew in a few short years from an evangelistic, quasi-Buddhist cult into a huge semi-religious, semi-military organization which is now assuming significant political status. Its members number in the millions, and they are dutiful voters. The Soka Gakkai philosophy is an ancient one based on the only Buddhist sect which was, like Christianity, intolerant of all other religions. Strong personal pressure is used to force persons to join the organization, which is administered by a system of block leaders in a manner reminiscent of Nazism. This cult offers solace to the lonely and lost individuals who are to be found in any country undergoing such rapid changes as those now taking place in Japan. Yet, politically, it apparently appeals to a good many people besides the lost and lonely. Through its political arm, Komeito, or Clean Government Party, Soka Gakkai is the third largest force in Japanese government today, holding the balance of power in the Tokyo Metropolitan Assembly after siphoning votes away from both Socialists and Liberal-Democrats. Some Japanese government officials believe that if Komeito succeeds in developing a secular image dissociated from the fanaticism of

Soka Gakkai, it may well be running the country within a few years. Soka Gakkai will, of course, still be behind it.

Whether it achieves the great heights predicted for it remains to be seen. It is likely that the even greater organization that is Japanese society will remain strong enough in its traditions so that none of the new cults, not even Soka Gakkai, will rise to dangerous power. At any rate, the Japanese people do not want another experience with militaristic fanaticism.

What *do* they want? In their present national mood, the Japanese people want things, material things. They do not altogether understand the Westerner's delight in Japanese ways of living. In the old days the Japanese people had few wants, or, more correctly, they refrained from wanting what they could not afford. Frugality was not considered a hardship but a dignified way of life, an idea strongly encouraged by the lords and masters. Now, except in the back country where old ideas and standards still prevail, austerity is giving way to relative affluence, and with the change, new wants are being discovered. A revolution of expectations is in progress. This is not to say the revolution is an immodest one, by American standards. A car is still a luxury item, and though most homes have television, most, also, have septic tanks. The Japanese work hard, go to bed early, and do well on the yen equivalent of a hundred to a hundred and fifty dollars per month. But their bursting vitality, now concentrated on achieving "the good life" instead of armament and empire, is carrying them fast along the road Americans have already traveled. May the gods of Asia have mercy!

Yet even more than things, the Japanese want peace, above all else, *peace.* They feel strongly on two points besides—namely, trade with Red China, and the status of Okinawa. They accept the present state of their homeland, American bases everywhere, and even their trouble with Russia over the northern islands and the fishing grounds. But they are not satisfied or even quiescent about Red China and Okinawa.

Japan is, after all, an Asian nation with Asian habits of thought. There is a strong feeling of racial and cultural affinity for the Chinese, and satisfaction that China has succeeded in throwing off European—which means, to them, Russian—domination. There is also a leaning toward Marxism and socialism on the part of many Japanese intellectuals, who turned to the left in opposition to prewar militarism, and have never changed since then. Of course the Liberal-Democratic government goes along with the West on China policy but, while refusing to recognize Peking, Japan is, unofficially, increasing trade and cultural relations with the Communists. They do not believe that mainland China threatens Japan and they do believe China's fanatical Marxism will eventually become more moderate.

As for Okinawa, the political fact that nobody will deny is that Okinawans wish once again to become part of Japan, and Japan is in total sympathy with them. The more serious thinkers among the Japanese and Okinawans recognize and appreciate that whereas the Russians expelled all Japanese from the Kuriles and have made the islands part of Soviet territory, the United States has allowed Japan to retain residual sovereignty over the Ryukus, or Okinawa. They also realize that American airfields in Okinawa are essential for the defense of the free peoples, but they cannot see why the government in Okinawa must remain with the American military forces. What adds to, rather than diminishes, their resentment is the knowledge that when the day comes for the departure of the American military forces, many Okinawans will be without means of livelihood.

That there is some cause for ill will cannot be denied. The arable land on Okinawa is scanty at best. Now much of it lies eternally buried under the miles of solid cement required for the great airfields. Yes, the farmers were paid for their land, but they were displaced, nevertheless. They are no longer independent landowners. They and their sons and daughters have become employees of the American military and servants for American families. Thus their resentment, and thus their unease. The large number of children born of Okinawan women but fathered by American men adds to the present discontent and fear of the future. It is understood by the Japanese that Okinawa will be returned to them, but who knows when? Meanwhile they fervently hope that the new command there, as of 1966, will be more democratic and less militaristic than the previous command. One hopes with them that the causes for present discontent will soon be wiped away.

XV

Yes, we still have difficulties to resolve. It is surprising that we have so few, after all the years of bitterness. In the past each people approached the other in ignorance and enmity. An attack such as was made upon Pearl Harbor is not reasonless. It is the result of ignorance, lack of understanding and consequent long, slow-growing hate. Westerners were unjust in many ways in their dealings with the Japanese people. Out of their smoldering resentments there came one day the explosion of war.

After the war, however, came the amazing occupation and the mutual discovery of the two peoples. It is astonishing to see how greatly our relationship has changed. The enforced living together of Japanese and Americans during occupation days brought about such a friendship as might never have been otherwise achieved. Because of it our two peoples understand each other as never before. I believe that the Japanese now think of us as the Westerners that they like the best. We, in our turn, like the Japanese and feel we know them more than any other Asian people. I have spoken of change in them, but there has been as great a change in us. At last we are beginning to know something of Asia, and our new knowledge is permeating our lives whether we realize it or not. The many thousands of servicemen and their families have brought back something of value, including a perspective that had been lacking before. Both of us have gained immeasurably by the meeting of our vastly different cultures. I think that we are now seeing the Renaissance of the twentieth century. Neither of us will ever be the same again, and I say this gratefully. We have become more like each other.

This does not mean, however, that either people has changed its basic characteristics. Perhaps the Japanese are becoming more democratic and we are becoming a little less so, but the fact remains that the Japanese people are not really democratic at all. In spite of democratization in many areas of life, they still have no real feeling of brotherhood, no true belief in the equality of man. They are accustomed to the idea of an elite and I think they always will be. There is still that difference between the upper and the lower classes, still the belief in the rightness of the hierarchical system. They have no idea at all of giving up their emperor; stripped of divinity though he may be, he is still the head of state and a revered figure. Nevertheless, their form of government, today, is democratic.

How much are the Japanese and the Americans alike? More than one could guess! We are alike in our curiosity about the world, about life, about anything new. We share a common devotion to sport, we are both ready for change, even to changing our minds about each other. We are both dedicated to science and the scientific method. We Americans share with Japan ideals of individual dignity and worth, of freedom and democratic government, of law and order and self-discipline. Above all, we share a desire for peace.

It would be interesting to explore the reach of the influences exchanged between the two peoples, and yet for the most part they are quite obvious. Architecturally, for example, the exchange is in skyscraper business houses in Japan and private homes in the United States—elevators and shoji! In fashions, gardens, arts, all sorts of household and electrical equipment, scientific theories and accomplishments, there is mutual exchange and benefit. In many ways, Japanese and American ways of doing things have permeated each other with influence. This morning, for example, waking at about six, I turned on my bedside radio—a Japanese transistor, by the way—to catch the early news. It was before the hour and I listened to music. What did I hear? In the midst of popular American melodies I heard popular Japanese melodies sung to a Japanese two-stringed violin, and this without explanation and quite as a matter of course! Instantly I was reminded of that evening in Tokyo, when my host took me to see the huge rock-and-roll theater. There they were, the young Japanese singers with their long hair, twanging their guitars and singing American folk songs, and there were the Japanese girls in the audience, screaming and applauding exactly as their counterparts do in the United States. Whether one approves or not is not the question. However one may report a certain loss, there is a preponderant gain. The divisions in the human race are ceasing to be national and racial. Perhaps the ideological is no great improvement, but in time that too can be solved, if one accepts humanity as a whole.

What is important to us here and now is that, in spite of insular history, philosophy and psychology, the Japanese more than any other Asian people have chosen to modernize, to transistorize, to rise with spectacular speed to great-nation status. Now to our mutual benefit and growing friendship we are developing a unique relationship through trade. The trade exchange between our two peoples maintains and abets a cultural exchange greater than has ever before existed between any two nations of the East and West. The influence of the West upon Japan is likely to spread throughout Asia, a fact of immeasurable importance to us.

In spite of such exchange and interchange, I repeat that our two peoples, although mutually influenced and influencing, remain basically true to our national and traditional characteristics. Americans still tend to think of Japan as exotic, delicate, artistic, charming. Certainly they have these traits in some areas. But in other areas they are strong, competitive, intelligent, modern. They are a masculine people rather than feminine. Emotional though they are, they are logical and decide by reason, necessity and profit.

Take, for example, the matter of industry. The people of Japan recognize with full appreciation the generosity with which the American government and American businessmen have aided and protected Japanese industry in the postwar recovery of Japan. The last impression they would want to make would be one of ingratitude. Nevertheless, in their rapid development they are approaching the acute moment of real competition with their benefactors. They are becoming rivals to the very men who have been their protectors. This troubles the Japanese very much. Yet the moment is near, indeed it has come, when the competition must be recognized, let markets fall where they may. American industry is already protesting and tariffs are rising, in echo of the old inequalities. The Japanese have adhered heroically to American policy in regard to trade and communication with China, but if tariffs and trade with the United States become too difficult, inevitably Japan must renew her Chinese markets in order to maintain her economy. Ideologies cannot stand where livelihood and business interests are concerned. Fortunately the people of the United States are themselves a practical people and are fully aware that competitors, balancing profit and loss, must learn to give and take. Thus industry and trade agreements are a relatively easy area in which to negotiate.

Far more difficult to adjust are matters of policy. The fact is that the Japanese people have now arrived at full maturity as a modern nation and are aware of it. It is natural and inevitable that they are determined to be treated as equals by all other peoples, including Americans. In delicacy, they remember the generosity with which they have been treated, they are grateful because they are fair and courteous, but they are also resolute and determined to be independent in their beliefs as well as their actions. Ever since defeat and the atomic bomb, they have had a strong sense of mission in the modern world. They see themselves as peacemakers and mediators. Therefore they believe in neutralism. For Americans neutralism is a colorless passivity. For the Japanese neutralism is moral courage and spiritual independence.

Their neutralism flared into active protest over the United States Security Treaty which allows us military bases on Japanese soil, and the feeling against the situation is still strong in the hearts of the Japanese people. I was in Japan at the time the treaty was negotiated and I saw the sharp protests that took place. It was a startling experience to see the streets of Tokyo swelling with crowds of angry people, mainly university students—always a significant sign, for in the articulateness of students the feelings of the people find vent. This demonstration was in support of the constitution which the Americans themselves had given to the Japanese; they had accepted this constitution so warmly that they were protesting in its defense. It seemed to them that the United States itself was violating its own declarations for peace in setting up the postwar bases. In fairness to the Japanese, I must say that, contrary to reports in Western newspapers, the students were not anti-American. I came and went on the streets of Tokyo during the so-called riots, without the slightest mishap. The Japanese people had not, and have not, changed their minds about liking Americans. No, the truth is that those crowding, pushing Japanese students, massing in protest against the rearmament of Japan, were in fact demanding to remain what the Americans had insisted they become, a people forswearing military arms and ways, a people forsaking the ways of the past, a people dedicated to peace, after the atomic bomb. Is this not another of Japan's contradictions?

It is true that there are Japanese individuals and even groups who do not believe in neutralism as a foreign policy, but the far greater force is the deep spiritual emotion which urges the people toward peace. This postwar attitude of the Japanese people is of enormous value to us. We need peace, we need their friendship. Today the people of Japan, so eminently Asian in all past centuries, have chosen to ally themselves with the people of the West. I repeat, our most bitter enemy in Asia has become our best friend there.

We will always find, in the people of Japan, paradoxes, inconsistencies and contrasts. We will see signs of change, and then discover upon closer scrutiny that it is not change so much as adaptation to a changing world. We will be baffled many times as we learn to know each other better. Yet we cannot make things easier for ourselves by deciding to accept modern Japan only. The people of Japan live in history and today. The Grand Shrine of Izumo at Shimane is neither more nor less truly Japanese than is the modern Sakuma dam project that has curbed the turbulent river Tenryu to provide electric power for Tokyo and Nagoya. The Kosakais of the back country are not more truly Japanese than the Yamaguchis of the business world. The modern scientists of Japan who have contributed so much to the world's knowledge and have indeed become the leaders in the area of the ionosphere, are no less Japanese than the famous poet of centuries ago who used the strict, traditional seventeen-syllable form of haiku to write with cheerful cynicism:

Dancing girls
Are always
Nineteen years old.

It is this contrast between old and new, sometimes violent, usually subtle, which makes Japan one of the most interesting countries in the world, a country to reckon with in this age when, as never before, East and West are searching for each other, in mutual dread of combat, and in mutual hope for a cooperative peace.

These, then, are my thoughts about the people I love, the people of Japan. They are a great people, unique in their ability to change and grow, while they maintain their traditional national integrity, and almost evangelistic in their desire for peace. The most modern people in Asia, and our best friends there, they stand in a strategic position between East and West, a place of power and influence for peace and for the welfare of mankind.

In this age, I say, the people of Japan have a unique opportunity, even a mission, to stand between the two halves of the world as interpreter and friend.